SEVEN STEPS TO EXPORT SUCCESS
FOR BUSINESSES THAT WON'T LET
BREXIT STOP THEIR GLOBAL GROWTH

# EXPORT.
# THRIVE.
# CHANGE THE
# WORLD

GW00503454

## Jennifer Claire Robson

# Export. Thrive. Change the World

## Seven Steps To Export Success For Businesses That Won't Let Brexit Stop Their Global Growth

**Jennifer Claire Robson**

## Export. Thrive. Change the World

Published by
The Endless Bookcase
Available from: www.theendlessbookcase.com

The Endless Bookcase
71 Castle Road, St Albans, Hertfordshire, England UK, AL1 5DQ

**Printed Edition**
Also available in multiple e-book formats.

# Acknowledgements

You pick up a book and flip to the acknowledgements and find once again that the author has dedicated the book to someone else not you.

Not this time

This one is for you.

I sincerely hope that it helps you on your journey to export success.

# About the Author

## Jennifer Claire Robson

I'm Jennifer Robson, author of Export. Thrive. Change the World: For businesses that won't let Brexit stop their global growth.

I have spent 10 years working in the export sector, spanning the UK, Europe and Asia. During that time I developed my seven steps to export success, which I will share with you in this book.

I've seen first-hand the benefits that come from the exchange of ideas and business opportunities across borders. But I've also experienced the frustration of red tape, lack of available knowledge and resulting missed opportunities.

In 2015 I decided to change that by setting up my own consultancy – Routes & Branches. I help British SMEs explore exporting opportunities by using the Seven Steps (www.routesandbranches.com) that I believe are fundamental to export success and growth.

My career began as a parliamentary researcher, then policy advisor and a working group member to encourage a greater exchange of expertise between British and Dutch businesses.

Based in The Hague, I became a Trade Advisor for UK Trade & Investment, identifying and securing opportunities for British SMEs to do business in the Netherlands. A move to Asia resulted in me leading the Business Services team at the British Chamber of Commerce in Singapore. In this role, I helped more than 450 companies to develop their export strategy and business capabilities in Singapore.

I've since moved to India, another vibrant and booming business market. My knowledge of exporting is steeped in on-the-ground experience in multiple markets, all vastly different from my hometown of Leeds.

# Reviews

*"I liked the 'voice' of the book and I could appreciate the comments about the way Women in business see various challenges of exporting."*
**Helen Akiyama Japanese - English language & cultural specialist at <u>Akiyamaconnects.co.uk</u>**

*"A practical and considered guide to understanding how to be a successful exporter as a British business owner. The book is full of really helpful questions and information. If you need advice on preparing for exporting then, Jenny is your one-stop shop for guidance and consultancy to make exporting a success for your business".*
**Ekua Cant: Founder of Drinksbot**

*"Love the book and the ideas in it"... I think this book is amazing!"*
**Barbara Hollyhead Chartered Marketer BA (Hons) MCIM DipM DipCAM (DigitalM)**
**Agave BlueMarketing  <u>www.agavebluemarketing.com</u>**

# Preface

I want to help you.

If you have picked up this book, you are probably a small to mid-size British business owner looking to create a thriving business that makes meaningful change in the world.

Exporting might seem like the logical way to grow, but it can also feel intimidating and well outside of your comfort zone, particularly with Brexit looming. I'm here to open your eyes to the potential that awaits you and make it less daunting in the process.

This book explains the clarity you need before you decide to export, with plenty of resources to guide you through the process. If you decide exporting is for you, I'd welcome you onto my course (www.routesandbranches.com) that teaches you step-by-step how to become an exporter. Thereafter I work one-on-one with clients to turn their exporting dreams into reality.

I hope you will be one of them.

Jennifer

# Contents

# Introduction

This book has a rather provocative title on purpose, I aim to challenge the 99% of businesses in the UK that are classified as SME or micro businesses to prepare their business for export and in doing so to change the world.

I intend to provide them with the tools and resources to be able to do so. Brexit has barely left the UK and international news since Theresa May invoked article 50 on the 29th March 2017. But in my opinion, Brexit is one of many issues that is preventing enough UK businesses from Exporting.

So what is the purpose of this book? My purpose is to demonstrate to UK business owners that they can use export as a mechanism to build thriving sustainable businesses and in doing so they will tackle and overcome some of the biggest challenges the world faces today. I'm publishing at the time the UK has invoked article 50 and is about to separate from the EU. A pivotal point in the UK's history. Brexit has opened up a dialogue about our values and vision and given us a great opportunity to change the course of our nation.

I'm going to split the book into three sections. The first will address the necessary paradigm shift in our thinking; the second will identify the five major challenges that are holding UK exporters back in the current economic climate. Section three is more cheery and aims to help you the British business owner embark on your journey to successful export and overcome the five challenges identified. I will guide you through my Seven steps that I believe are fundamental to export success and business growth.

After ten years in the export sector both working for the Government Department for International Trade and then as the founder of Routes and Branches limited www.routesandbranches.com my export consultancy company I decided it was time to "write up" my observations into a book and in doing so record my process for helping UK companies to export successfully.

I'm making the assumption that if you have picked up my book it's because you are interested in developing a thriving international business and want to understand how to do this in an effective and sustainable way.

What I have come to realise is that the economic models used globally are serving the few not the many. Causing a crisis of resources and in many places political unrest and it is set to get worse. Collectively we have assumed that GDP is king we have built our economies and our businesses on growth rather than looking at how we can thrive. Exporting for growth is not working. Not enough of us are doing it. Each time we grow the goal posts move further away as we seek to grow further. The more and more we push on the more people we leave behind and the more destruction we cause for our environment.

Exporting doesn't need to be a mechanism for growth it can be a mechanism to promote thriving global economies, sustainability and care. Kate Raworth has developed an economic model to create thriving regenerative and distributive economies (Kate Raworth, 2018). I believe her model is possible and in reach, if we adjust our thinking, let go of our assumptions and reformulate our values. I believe that if we utilise export as a mechanism to connect ideas and command attention that we can realise the Raworth model and change the world.

The first step is to change our businesses and access export as a mechanism for development.

So let's start with the core principle that all successful businesses have three things in common:

1. Something to sell,

2. That something has to solve a problem or be desirable to people so that they want to buy it,

3. Once customers have bought it, it has to be so good that they want to recommend it to others.

If you don't have something to sell then you are not ready for export. Go back to the drawing board. Develop a product test it in your domestic market and refine it until you can be sure that it is

a. Solving a problem.
b. Desirable to consumers.
c. So good that consumers want to recommend it to others.

If you have decided to sell someone else's product or service you need to ensure that that too meets the criteria above.

So assuming that you meet these three criteria, how do you ensure export success? How do you overcome the major challenges holding UK companies back?

Before I even get started on discussing why Brexit might hold exporters back let's look at some of the other major issues at play. In this book I have identified the five major challenges that I believe hold British Business back and prevent them from exporting; here they are in a nutshell:

1. We (British businesses) are so small.

2. Service accounts for 74%.

3. Businesses are dying before they mature.

4. Failure to plan.

5. Brexit.

I am going to look at each of these five elements in the context of Kate Raworth's economic paradigm that "Tomorrows thriving future must be growth agnostic". (Kate Raworth, 2017)

It is my hope and aspiration that reading this book will give you a clear understanding of whether or not your business is export ready and that using the book will help prepare you for export success.

# Section 1: A paradigm shift

I've written this book from the perspective that you like me believe that now is the time for a major shift in our thinking. In the wake of Brexit, we (British citizens) need to go back to our values as a nation and re-establish our place in the world. In doing so we the British public need to step up and lead the way "to be the change we wish to see in the world" (Mahatma Gandhi). We have to be brave. To step out of our comfort zones and begin to address the challenges that lie before us with creative balanced solutions that benefit not just us as an individual, company, or even country but us as a global society of interconnected human beings. That is my big vision.

It starts with shifting our economic outlook away from the capitalist demands of maximum growth towards a more balanced, regenerative, and distributive economy that enables all people/life to thrive regardless of where they are in the world. To reference Mark Manson "we need to prioritise our fu*ks". To decide as a nation what's important to us and how we want to shape our place on the global stage. In my search for a better economic approach, I discovered an economic theory called doughnut economics developed by Kate Raworth. "The essence of the doughnut: a social foundation of well being that no one should fall below, and an ecological ceiling of planetary pressure that we should not go beyond. Between the two lies a safe and just space for all." (Raworth, 2017). Kate's theory has influenced my thinking and in this book I use it to frame my thoughts and guide some of my questions to exporters.

You will notice throughout the book that I leave unanswered questions with the hope of provoking you to think beyond your current boundaries to the possibilities for business success that exist if we (UK businesses) start to operate on a global level inclusive of all.

## What is doughnut economics?

For over two hundred years, industry has been based on degenerative design: we (humans) take Earths materials, make them into products we want then throw those products away. It's a one-way system that runs against Earth's cyclic processes of life. And it is destroying the planet's living systems on which we fundamentally depend.[i]

Contrary to the promises of the late-twentieth century economic theory, economic growth won't simply clean up the mess it makes. Which is why we (society) have to make our economies regenerative by design, so that Earth's materials can be used again and again. Figuring out how to do so is one of the greatest design challenges for twenty-first-century architects, industrialists, entrepreneurs, financiers, citizens and states. Achieving sustainable thriving economies means ensuring that all people have the resources needed such as food water, healthcare and energy to fulfil their human rights. We need to create economies that are local to global and bring all of humanity into the doughnuts safe and just space. The doughnut points towards a future that can provide for every person's needs whilst safeguarding the living world on which we all depend. (Raworth, Doughnut Economics: Seven Ways to Think Like a 21st-Century Economist, 2017).

In her book Doughnut economics, Kate sets our seven ways to think like a 21st-century economist.

1. Change the goal

2. See the big picture

3. Nurture human nature

4. Get savvy with systems

5. Design to distribute

6. Create to regenerate

7. Be agnostic about growth

I will come back to these concepts at various points in my book to help to illustrate the ways in which export can be used as a mechanism to help businesses to thrive.

I don't know about you but I find challenges illustrated by doughnut economics exciting, and I want to work with the companies who look at these challenges and see the possibility and promise of a thriving business.

It won't be easy. The challenge is complex and some of the boundaries are interdependent. Environmental stress can exacerbate poverty and vice versa.

But the positive news is that available data suggests that the minimum social foundation could be achieved with very few resources.

- Take food, for example, Just 1% of the current global food supply would provide the extra calories needed by the 13% of the world's population facing hunger.
- For less than a 1% increase in $CO_2$ emissions electricity could be brought to the 19% of the world's population who currently lack it.
- Ending income poverty for the 21% of the global population who live on less than $1.25 a day would require just 0.2% of global income. (Kate Raworth)

Human rights advocates have long highlighted the imperative of ensuring every person's claim to life's essentials while ecological economists have emphasised the need to situate the economy within environmental limits. The doughnut economics framework puts the two together, creating a closed system that is bound by both human rights and environmental sustainability.

The framework opens up three perspectives:

- **An integrated vision:** the interconnectedness of social, environmental and economic dimensions of sustainable development
- **Refocused economic priorities:** The economies overarching aim is no longer economic growth for

growth sake but to bring humanity into the safe and just space

- **Metrics beyond GDP:** Policymakers must be much more accountable for the impact of economic activity on planetary and social boundaries.

## Brexit: Our opportunity to change the world

As the UK prepares for a Brexit deal or non-deal (another prospect on the cards as I write) what we are actually coming to terms with is the interconnectedness of our societies and how to address the needs of our nation. Brexit is a trigger for change. Change processes are often uncomfortable and often face significant scrutiny. Let's explore the change we have requested so that we can focus on the impact it will have on exporters.

From a policy perspective, we have asked our government to perform an enormously complex task in very little time. Brexit will impact upon every single piece of legislation in every single sector. We (the public) are expecting them (the government) to keep the country and economy running smoothly whilst also wiping the slate clean and changing everything. There is a disconnect between those two demands. On the one hand, we want a break from Europe and to have more control of our own governance and on the other hand we want free and fair trade across borders. In order to change we will firstly move closer to Europe in policy terms. Parliament has legislated to repeal the ECA with the European Union (Withdrawal) Act 2018, which will convert all existing EU-derived law into domestic law. The Government's approach will allow the UK to decide over time what laws it wishes to retain and is intended to avoid the significant gaps and consequent uncertainty if all EU-derived law was repealed without replacement Parliament has legislated to repeal the ECA with the European Union (Withdrawal) Act 2018, which will convert all existing EU-derived law into domestic law. The Government's approach will allow the UK to decide over time what laws it wishes to retain and is intended to avoid the significant gaps and consequent uncertainty if all EU-derived law was repealed without replacement. (Norton Rose Fullbright) The key impact for Exporters here is it is unknown how long it will take to repeal and revise EU laws and what the impact on different sectors will be. The government are attempting to reduce the economic and commercial impacts in the short term by adopting existing EU legislation into UK law but in order to meet the peoples wishes and honour the results of the referendum subsequent changes to individual pieces of legislation will need to be made. Thus the long-term impact of Brexit will be significant and far-reaching.

Commercially, even if the UK decided not to retain any EU law, companies looking to trade in the EU would nevertheless still be required to comply with EU laws such as EU competition rules, regulations and standards.

So as a starting point exporters need to ensure that they are compliant with existing EU law. That they are aware of which laws are directly affecting their business and that they find channels and mechanisms such as the FSB, Chambers of Commerce, IOD to utilise to express their concerns and wishes when changes to specific pieces of legislation begin to be made. Now is the time to step up and participate, not watch from the sidelines.

The EU (Withdrawal) Act contains wide-ranging powers to amend EU-derived law by secondary legislation. In the Government's view, these powers will give sufficient scope to correct or remove laws that would otherwise not function properly after Brexit, although the Government has sought to stress that the powers will not be able to be used to create 'the new policy'. (Norton Rose Fullbright) The development of new trade policies affecting exporters is likely to be the second phase. The new policy will have to go through our normal parliamentary processes involving the Commons and the Lords. A bill can take anything from a couple of days to several years to pass through parliament but typically most bills pass through the parliamentary process within a year. Exporters should therefore expect change to be gradual over several years.

I will discuss the impacts of Brexit on exporters throughout the book.

## My Vision for a changed world post Brexit

My belief is that Brexit presents a great opportunity for more SME's to expand internationally.

My vision is for us (Business owners and entrepreneurs) to create a thriving global economy and society. I believe export is a mechanism and a process to help us to extend our reach and grow our audience so that we can maximise the impact of our solutions. Are the gains from export unequally distributed in society? Or does export facilitate more sustainable distribution of resources? I'm writing from the perspective that export is a mechanism that can support the regenerative redesign of our economies and societies. That it is a facilitator of value sharing and can help propel us to realise a more integrated vision. The regenerative design of our economies, supported by export will change the world.

In fact, I'd go so far as to say that we have a responsibility to export to give audience to our solutions, visions and values that will create a global way of operating that supports our planet and the people on it to thrive. I founded Routes and Branches on this basis as I felt it was necessary to use the skills I had developed at UKTI and the Chamber of Commerce to practically assist as many UK SME's as possible to expand internationally and create thriving businesses.

What does it mean to thrive?

The currency of the future is attention. In order to thrive, we (UK businesses) will need to capture and hold the attention of our customers, financers and employees. As brands we will need to both capture and immerse our audience. Business owners need to understand that attention breaks down into two pieces: intensity and duration. Intensity is the quality of the attention and duration is the quantity of it (Social Media Week, 2016). International brands will need to develop international marketing strategies that enable us to capture both intensity and duration of our audience's attention. I believe British business owners can do this by ensuring that we dedicate enough of our attention to the ecological ceiling and the social foundation, in other words, the big issues that capitalists economics are grappling with but that doughnut economics begins to address. I believe the ecological ceiling and social foundation is something business owners should prioritize.

Eleven social priorities have been identified as a result of the Millennium Development Goals and subsequent research and discussions leading to Rio+20. These eleven   priorities can be group into three distinct groups and are as follows:

1. **Well:** through food security, adequate income, improved water and sanitation, and healthcare.

2. **Productive:** through education, decent work, modern energy services, and resilience to shocks.

3. **Empowered:** through gender equality, social equality and having a political voice.

International marketing in a thriving global economy will not be easy. In fact, sometimes it's hard to know where to begin. There are a million and one things to do, and it feels incredibly overwhelming, confusing and sometimes even helpless. One of the ways that business owners can prevent ourselves from becoming overwhelmed by the sheer number of issues that we face is to identify our values and vision for our businesses and ourselves. I talk more about this in the next few chapters, but for now, I'd like to leave you with a thought to consider.

Businesses make very little impact by striving to solve the same issue in an overcrowded market. Instead, our efforts should be focused on the issues that are big, neglected and solvable. It is my belief that successful business owners will seek out the problems that others are systematically missing and seek out the markets that others are neglecting. Successful business owners will also play the long game and question themselves in the following way: (www.80000hours.org).

Would you choose to:

- Prevent one person from suffering next year or
- Prevent one hundred people from suffering one hundred years from now?:

The same can be applied to a business scenario, do you focus your attention on building one sale next month or one hundred sales in next year?

I don't want to just list out the problems. I want us to take a minute to pause and reflect on;

1. What impact these issues are having on our business?

2. What impact our businesses are having on these problems?

3. Are business owners comfortable with this status quo? What are we as individual business owners going to do about it? What are we as business owners going to focus our attention on?

## Brexit an opportunity for change, not fear

In my opinion, Brexit is a trigger that is shaking up the UK. Some may call it "the awakening it needs to realise that we have lost sight of our values and we have lost sight of our vision and sense of purpose and belonging in the world". I don't believe we (The UK) have lost our belonging but I do believe that we are in need of revisiting our values and better communicating our vision. That the vision should be a collective one shared by the whole population and a vision for our future that is ambitious, imaginative and inspiring. One that will enable us to confidently stand up for our beliefs, protect our people and preserve our environment. A vision of a thriving nation.

As the UK goes through the Brexit process what we are really doing as a country is having a conversation about what matters to us as a society and what our place is within the world. This is a big conversation with far-reaching consequences. We are collectively determining what matters to us, and what we want to focus our efforts on. One way or another our decisions will change the world.

As British citizens, we can be either swept along by the politicians and retrench rules and regulations that don't look and feel too different from the EU system we asked to move away from, or we can step up and assert ourselves. Lay our cards on the table and identify what values and vision we stand for, and then do the harder job of entrenching this vision in a series of processes that will govern our relationship with the rest of the world.

I am writing from the perspective that you my readers regardless of how you voted, view Brexit as an opportunity for change and are ready to embrace the change and the potential to thrive that comes with it. I personally voted to remain and had concerns from the offset that the leave campaign misled the general public and manipulated them with campaigns such as "we send the EU £350m a week, let's fund our NHS instead" (Financial Times) which many economists at the time argued was completely unrealistic. I thought that EU reform was necessary but believed that we were better equipped to do it from within rather than from the outside. However the majority of the British public did not share my view and the remain team lost the election. I strongly believe in democracy and the democratic process. The election was conducted freely and fairly and had a record turnout. So it is right for me to accept the outcome and seek the positives. In writing this book I hope to show you (Business owners) positive impacts of Brexit for your business regardless of how you voted.

Bonus: Visit my blog https://routesandbranches.com/brexit-business-opportunities/ to read or watch my video demystifying the government's white paper for exporters.

So now I'd like to talk to you about the five challenges that I can see are preventing British Businesses from thriving internationally. The fifth is Brexit. In my opinion all are challenges but all are solvable. But perhaps we are focusing our efforts on number five "Brexit" and neglecting the other four.

# Section 2: The five challenges holding UK businesses back from exporting

To set this chapter in context I would like to provide some insights into my own experiences and elaborate on how and why I chose to highlight these particular five issues. I began my career in the UK Houses of Parliament where my role was to advise on new policy and bills to pass through parliament. Many of the projects I worked on were a reflection of the views of small businesses in the Midlands (my MP's Constituency). During that period I worked with companies struggling to finance their small business, meet planning regulations, and in some cases expand internationally. My parliamentary role wetted my appetite for working with business but first I wanted to explore the democratic process and check for myself that my theoretical understanding of democracy was being reflected on the ground. I joined the UK Electoral Commission and became a Policy Advisor responsible for analysing the EU Parliamentary election and then UK Parliamentary election. Working at the Electoral Commission restored my faith in our democracy and the democratic process and gave me a chance to explore the impact of referendums from a theoretical perspective. I hope I am able to share this grounding with you in my exploration of Brexit and the impact it has on your business.

From the Electoral Commission I went to the Netherlands to join UKTI in the British Embassy in The Hague. The Netherlands and Benelux are major export markets for UK SME's and attract businesses of all sizes. It is during my time there that I first began to explore the concept of size of business being associated with export success. As the lead advisor for professional services and ICT I also made it my mission to challenge the assumption that services businesses can't and don't export. Which is why I chose number 2! Number 3 saddens me but is a reality that I have come across time and time again; Business leaders with great ambitions fail to sustain their businesses for a number of reasons, many die before they mature. I will elaborate based on my experiences.

Number 4 is about planning and resources; I've met many Business owners with ideas but no plan. I've made it my mission to help them plan and more importantly help them to implement their plans. I would say that this is a core element of the support we offer at Routes and Branches and definitely one of my motivations for creating my Routes course which guides business owners through my seven-step export success process.

Finally, Brexit, which in the current climate can't be ignored. I've been warned about tackling something so topical in my book as it "could disappear as a passing trend" however, I believe Brexit is a fundamental change in our political history, a significant expression of democracy and a huge opportunity to shape our future. Progress is not made without adversity. Some of the most successful exporters I've worked with have had to overcome significant challenges to thrive, from million pound engineering projects to cast steel bolts for offshore platforms that could sustain underwater environmental pressures, to injection moulding companies tasked with building a mould to construct a famous vacuum companies patented technology. I can give hundreds of other examples but in each case, the difference between success and failure boiled down to my seven steps and that is what I will share with you in the rest of this book.

## Challenge 1: Are UK Businesses too small to thrive?

In 2017, there were 5.7 million businesses in the UK. 99% of which are classified as small and medium-sized (SME's). 96% or 5.5 million were classified as micro businesses employing 0-9 people. SMEs account for 60 to 70 per cent of jobs in most OECD countries. Clearly, they are integral to the global economy. But are the government creating the right conditions to enable them to thrive?

Before I even start to think about the challenges associated with Brexit I need to address the challenges associated with having such a large number of very small businesses. As I mentioned I first began thinking about the challenge of scale whilst working as a Trade Advisor in the Hague. I had four burning questions:

- Are these businesses too small to thrive?
- Are they too small to make an impact and address the big global problems?
- Or can their size be used to their advantage?
- Is it just a question of correct positioning?

My work in the last 10 years has explored these questions and sought to answer them. Ninety per cent of the companies I work with employ less than fifty people and most average ten to fifteen employees. Each and every one of them is exporting. The majority are thriving. So I fundamentally believe that if you apply my seven-step approach to export success that you can thrive regardless of the size of your company. The first steps of my process are about creating a thriving UK business that can sustain export, this often means expanding your resources and capacity. So a solo entrepreneur or micro business is unlikely to export successfully without first thriving nationally. Don't be disheartened if this is the scale of your business right now. My seven-step process is your blueprint to success.

Perhaps the most fundamental question in this group seems to be "Are they too small to make an impact and address the big global problems?" I've come to the conclusion that most business owners hope to make a positive difference in the world.

To varying degrees, many of them do. But not all businesses are created equally. A business doesn't have to be community service-oriented to make a difference in the world. Whether through the services they deliver, their employment practices, or through their other activities, today's businesses have an impact on society. Exporting businesses have an impact upon a wider global society. That impact has the potential to change the world.

Different types of company deliver social change in different ways (Joel Comm). Let's have a look at how some of the different company structures deliver change and if these could be used overseas to help you to deliver your overseas mission.

- **Traditional non-profits:** non-profits exist to provide a service without making a profit. Any money these organizations make must be reinvested into the cost of furthering their mission.

- In America, businesses can register as **B-Corps**. B Corps meet a set list of requirements, including transparency in the socially-conscious work they do.
- **Mission-first companies** are oriented around a socially impactful mission, but operate as a for-profit enterprise.
- **Socially responsible businesses** may not put social impact first, but they realize the many benefits of being community-minded.
- The more traditional way to influence a social change is through donations.

Social impact initiatives are evolving. Small businesses realize they don't have to choose just one way to engage in community-minded activities. They can employ a blend. Many are using social impact to better meet their mission and help them further their brand reputation. Many small businesses apply business models that incorporate an element of community-minded activities into an otherwise very commercial arrangement.

Small exporting businesses are embarking on an exciting period of experimentation and innovation as they seek to advance their organisation's core objectives by addressing social and environmental issues. This is particularly true of the small businesses exporting to emerging markets and addressing the challenges associated with serving low-income consumers and rural communities (Deloitte, 2014).

Bonus: We discuss the advantages of being a small business https://routesandbranches.com/big-benefits-of-being-a-small-business/

*What do successful SME's have in common?*
Success isn't just about getting bigger it's often about having a mindset that is responsive to change. Having an unwavering belief in your values and purpose can help you persist in challenging times. You need a mindset that is pragmatic, accepting of failures and hungry for new knowledge and

improvement. This mind-set is fundamental. It's a concept I come back to in my book time and again and it is the very foundations of my seven-step approach.

There are ample opportunities for small businesses to do well while doing good. But making the business case for solving social needs requires a change in mind-set and new ways of doing business. The specific needs of underserved consumers, the social challenges facing local suppliers, and the limits of infrastructure and education require a sustained commitment to serve a particular market. This might require longer-term planning, changes in the product development process, new forms of collaboration, and innovative business models (Deloitte, 2014).

I've studied hundreds of SME's in the past ten years and worked with hundreds more. The successful ones share common traits.

Below I list some of the traits that SME's have in common:

- Likely to use more than one source of finance (Surrey University).
- They proactively monitor their cash flow.
- They consider direct referrals and search engine optimisation as central to their success.
- They are willing to find new ways of doing things
- They believe that learning gives them a competitive advantage.
- They are willing to seek advice.
- They are flexible and adapt to changing market conditions.

Perhaps it's useful to share with you an example of a company that was missing some of these traits. In my first year of Routes and Branches, I worked with a skincare company founded by an extremely ambitious and talented female entrepreneur. She had developed a fantastic product scientifically backed and proven to work. Her packaging was attractive and well designed. Her website was efficient and pleasing to the end user. But what she lacked was a reliable scalable source of finance. So when she began exporting she was unable to build credibility in the new market because she didn't have the mechanisms to scale at the rate that was required to deliver volumes that would make export make sense for the distributors. Unfortunately, without the ability to finance growth she was unable to adapt to the changing market conditions in the export market and unable to sustain repeat orders. Had she being more willing to find new ways of doing things we could have helped her to secure export financing or utilised banking tools to secure finance against her orders. My point is that it's important to have the right leaders with the right mind-set in order for export to succeed. If you have the right mind-set other challenges like financing can be overcome. We have a network of experts in all areas of export, including finance, logistics, compliance and can draw on this expertise to support your business to overcome any export challenge except mind-set. You have to work on that first. Which is why I start my seven steps with Vision and Values as these are fundamental frameworks for a success mind-set. If you understand your why you can thrive.

## Challenging assumptions

It is assumed that as a general rule of thumb the smaller the business is the less likely it is to export. "I'm a small business" or "I'm too small" are common sentiments expressed by business owners as a reason for not exporting (Federation of Small Business, 2016). Many small businesses are deterred by false assumptions that exporting is not for them. Women-owned businesses are particularly vulnerable to making this assumption.

The US small businesses administration claims that only 1% of American small businesses currently export overseas (Mcmahon). In comparison, a FedEx "SME Export Report (Startups UK)" says 63% of UK SME's are now exporting. So assuming that size is a barrier is naïve, British SME's are proving it can be done.

That's not to say that export is easy. Export by its very nature impacts upon every aspect of the business so can be a lot of work for a small team to handle. If you employ less than 10 people and are exporting successfully you can expect to have a very busy team.

Big impact comes from being able to answer three key questions:

1. Is the problem the business is trying to address big in scale?

2. Is the problem neglected?

3. Is the problem solvable?

I've noticed that the Small businesses and entrepreneurs that are thriving are the ones that are beginning to leverage technology and global marketplace platforms to reach consumers in new ways (World Bank). We have worked with several companies to help them leverage technology to facilitate export. One of the most memorable and certainly the most fun was a leather bag company who used Kickstarter to finance a digitization of their business which completely transformed their ability to sell overseas at scale. Prior to the digitization, they had literally brought clients to their factory from countries such as China to choose the leather and other bespoke elements of their bags. Not cost effective and not scalable. They partnered with a local digitization company to build a bespoke platform enabling customers anywhere in the world to select their design elements and have a custom bag made.

## How else are small businesses contributing to a thriving economy?

SME's are the launchers of new ideas. They assimilate processes. They accelerate the more efficient use of resources (Zaman, 1999). They are also an essential source of jobs and contribute two-thirds of all the new jobs added. But they also play another important role by reducing the capacity of big companies to control a market.

*How can you help yourself to export as a small business?*

Exporting is a huge step to take in business and, like all aspects of your journey, requires significant research and dedication. Expanding your service or product overseas can take your business to another level. If you're successful, it can transform it.

But if you are not ready it can be extremely damaging and in some cases fatal.

The first step is to make sure you are "Export ready". I have created an export readiness checklist which is available to download from my website (www.routesandbranches.com). I'll share some basic principles with you here;

1. You need to be successful in the UK first, spend time establishing a brand reputation for the right reasons.

2. Do thorough market research: I can't stress the importance of this one enough. You must make sure there is a demand for your product or service.

3. Research and understand the potential barriers and ask for help where you need it.

Firstly, get out of your own way. Stop it with the what if's. What if it doesn't work out? What if no one buys? What if I get the pricing wrong?

When you think of the what ifs you hold your business back, overthink everything and procrastinate.

What if I take the what ifs and flip them on their head?

What if it's an international bestseller? People love it. Everyone buys it. What if it goes better than you can ever imagine?

Still scared?

One of the ways that you can help yourself to export as a micro business owner is to sell your product or service to another UK business that exports. We can help you to identify appropriate business partners for your business. One of our most recent matches was to link an inventor to a printer. The printer has enough scale and is already exporting so was able to offer favourable financial terms to the inventor and take her product into wider markets without her having to purchase huge volumes of stock upfront.

Supply chains play an important role in a modern interconnected economy. For every £3 of value added generated domestically (in the UK) for exporting, £2 is generated directly by the exporting industry and £1 is generated by their UK based suppliers (UK Government). We have helped several SME's to leverage their supply chain to grow their business. This can take different formats. One company partnered with four others in their sector to leverage one logistics company so that they could send a complete twenty-foot container to market rather than several individual pallets. The five companies combined their shipments, saving them all time and money to reach market. The downside or risk of this approach though is the paperwork and ensuring that each part of the shipment is correctly categorised and accounted for.

Export support must begin to address these assumptions so that businesses don't fall at the first hurdle. One of my motivations to move from government into my own business was to practice what I preach and share my knowledge and tools to help address this concern and help more businesses to export. I provide a weekly blog and podcast to address the concerns of exporters and help them to explore opportunities in new markets. Please subscribe and leave a comment with your thoughts.

This is not necessarily a bad thing. Small, agile focused teams can make a significant impact in the world. I've worked with some really inspiring companies that are addressing challenges such as sanitary waste, how to reduce landfill, how to create water cooling systems to reduce energy bills, how to use vegetation bags to prevent landslide whilst also reducing road noise and pollution. I'm really privileged to work with small impactful businesses every day. To help them to plan for success, identify and link to the right partners be that supply chains or distribution channels or both; to be able to go in person to foreign markets and showcase their products for them and with them. At last count, I've visited thirty-two countries and lived in four. I'm not stating this to show off I'm stating this to demonstrate that we literally go the extra mile for our exporters taking them around the world and using our first-hand connections to expand their businesses. My connections span the globe and are real relationships built over a number of years. The most important aspect of my business is matching your business to the right partners. It's what separates me from my competition. Like a good house wine, it's what I'm staking my reputation on so it's hands-on relationship building and due diligence to make sure everyone I link to your business is someone I'd be willing to work within mine.

## Challenge 2: Assumption that Service businesses export less than manufactures.

The service industries accounted for 74% of businesses. In 2017 there are 4.3 million businesses in the service industry in the UK, or ¾ of all UK businesses. The biggest of the service industry in terms of number of businesses was professional, scientific and technical industry, which accounted for 15% of businesses.

In the past, it has been assumed that service businesses think less about exporting than product-based businesses. Perhaps this is because it feels less tangible to export a service than something you can physically see, touch and feel. The FSB demonstrated in their recent report that there is a common misunderstanding about what constitutes exporting. Many small businesses believe that exporting must involve a physical product and, therefore, intangible products such as services cannot be exported or count as an export product. (Federation of Small Business, 2016)

The UK manufacturing sector accounted for 5% of businesses in the UK. Manufacturers are the ones typically expected to export. But at such a low proportion of the overall economy, they can't make the governments export targets alone. Moving to the web makes a company more nimble and capable of responding to opportunities in international markets. Many traditional manufactured product exports increasingly contain technology that requires installation, troubleshooting, maintenance, and repairs (Trade Ready, 2016). Giving Service companies an opportunity to export in support of their manufacturing clients.

Service exports are an important emerging trend in global trade. The predominance of the Internet and cloud-based communication has enabled information related services to flow freely around the world. Companies that deliver web-based products and services, such as e-commerce, SaaS, PaaS, and consumer web and mobile, tend to experience turbocharged global growth, simply because they can take their software or website international without making a large investment.

### So what counts as a service export?

A service export is, very simply, any service provided by a resident in one country to people or companies from another (Trade Ready, 2016).

Many services are "exported" but never cross any physical boundaries. Many companies are already exporting services without realizing it!

### Does volume or method matter?

The FSB found that not all methods of selling might be perceived equally as exporting. (Federation of Small Business, 2016) More traditional methods of selling, such as shipping products overseas, tend to be seen as proper exporting rather than certain online methods, such as via platforms like Etsy. Other small firms that sell to customers abroad may not see themselves as exporting because their overseas trade is not the primary focus or mainstay of the business.

### What challenges are service businesses facing when exporting?

The first export challenge is to recognise what constitutes exporting.

Next for many services businesses is to move from a one-to-one business model to a one-to-many. Once this is achieved, normally through the creation of a web-based product. International markets become much more accessible.

The next challenge for service companies is compliance when selling across international borders. I have dedicated a chapter to legitimacy and discuss the ways in which businesses must become compliant in order to be legitimate.

Bonus: You can also visit my blog to watch my video on Compliance and legitimacy https://routesandbranches.com/business-export-success-07-exporting-compliance-legitimacy/

## Challenge 3: Businesses are dying before they mature

According to the Centre for Economics and Business Research CEBR, the UK is among the five worst performing countries in Europe when it comes to getting SME's exporting. (The Guardian , 2016) Perhaps one of the reasons for this is they die before they mature. There were 414,000 business births and 328,000 business deaths in 2015 (Webpresence digital). This has a major impact on export. Over half of UK businesses engaged in international trade in goods are at least ten years old. The FSB in a recent survey found that firms older than four years are more than twice as likely to export as start-ups (Federation of Small Business, 2016). If many of our companies fail before they reach ten years with that failure also goes export potential. The most likely group to export are small businesses aged between twenty and forty-nine years old.

More than half of new businesses in the UK don't survive beyond five years. Once up and running many business owners struggle to plan for the long term. Many lack confidence in their ability to achieve consecutive growth for their business. One of the ways we help small businesses is to provide advice and tips through our free resources, (blog, webinars, and podcast) these cover a range of subjects aimed at helping first-time exporters or those considering export to take the necessary steps to export successfully. We also encourage SME's to engage with us and ask questions on our social media platforms.

44% of SME business owners cite the UK tax system as their major concern. This is closely followed by lack of bank lending, and thirdly late payments and cash flow. (The Telegraph) Inadequate cash reserves and poor cash flow management is a significant contributor to the failure of UK SME's.

No matter what industry you operate in business failure tends to be the result of either lack of management skill or lack of capital.

There are eleven common causes of business failure

1. Choosing a business that isn't very profitable.

2. Inadequate cash reserves.

3. Failure to understand your market.

4. Failure to price correctly.

5. Failure to correctly anticipate cash flow.

6. Overgeneralization.

7. Over-dependence on a single customer.

8. Uncontrolled growth.

9. Believing you can do everything yourself.

10. Inadequate management.

11. Founder attitude.

Many businesses fail because they are started for the wrong reasons or their founder lacks a clear vision and values. To be successful you have to have a passion and drive for what you will be doing. You need to be really determined at times it will be incredibly difficult and if you lack a clear vision it will be easy to throw in the towel. Successful business owners are also lifelong learners constantly striving to improve and using their failures as lessons to reach the next level of business success. . I get excited when a client comes to me with a big vision, one such client gave me goosebumps as she announced that she wanted to have a million pound business by the time she was thirty. She's 27 we have three years. She's in the process of negotiating a multimillion-pound deal and has a series of other businesses successes including selling on Amazon, exporting to two countries and beating her 1st years' sales last month. I can work with big visions by breaking them down, asking why until the only answer left is why not! I turn big visions into reality through practical implementation plans and clear consistent processes. So no matter whether you have never exported or have several markets under your belt, I can help you to thrive.

Underestimating the difficulty of starting a business is one of the biggest obstacles entrepreneurs face. However, success can be yours if you are patient, willing to work hard, and take all the necessary steps.

As a society we need to be more accepting of business failure as positive creative destruction. Destruction is a creative force for productive growth. If something is failing to be cost effective or to meet market demands it goes out of business making space for better solutions. The more in tune business owners can be with the market the more chance they have of refining their product to meet market needs and thus stay in business. If they can apply this across multiple territories they can meet a wider range of needs and are far more likely to sustain the business for the longer term.

Smart business owners also focus their efforts on neglected areas where they have a much greater chance of making a bigger impact. They choose a market with growth potential and they do their market research in advance to make sure that the business they are building is not in a sector, which is stagnating or declining. . I've worked with a couple of business owners who came to me with a failing business that they lacked excitement for and we have ended up building something completely different based on their passion, knowledge and skills. Sometimes the best advice is knowing when to change.

A leading cause of business failure is overexpansion. Overexpansion (www.businessknowhow.com) often happens when business owners confuse success with how fast they can expand their business. A focus on slow and steady growth is optimum. Many a bankruptcy has been caused by rapidly expanding companies. This is one that exporters should be particularly conscious of. Make sure that you plan for success and plan the growth of your supply chain as well as your business. I have witnessed businesses fail because their supply chain didn't have the capacity to keep up with the scale of their growth. That's why as part of our growth strategies we perform due diligence on your supply chain to analyse their strengths and weaknesses and to look at opportunities for growth. You won't thrive if your supply chain fails so you need to carry them along with you, some of the big multinationals have found this out the hard way. Just google the day KFC ran out of chicken!

## The harsh reality

Many of our UK small, medium and micro sized businesses will fail. They will fail for a number of reasons but Brexit is unlikely to be the major cause. More likely is that they are not solving a problem big enough in scale. They are trying to solve a problem that too many others are trying to solve so there just isn't room for them in the market. Or (and this is the least likely) they are trying to solve a problem that isn't solvable.

As larger businesses fail they are often replaced by a larger number of smaller businesses or sole proprietorships. The number of sole proprietorships (businesses with no employees) has grown by more than the number of all businesses (by 84% compared to 59% for all businesses). Solo businesses are less likely than micro businesses to export. So it is no surprise that as the number of solo businesses raises the number of businesses who export decreases.

In recent years the UK has lagged behind many developed nations in the contributions SME's make to GDP (The Telegraph, 2015). One of my big concern is that British Business owners are not tapping into the potential of a global workforce. Therefore, not sharing the knowledge available to solve some of the global challenges we face. In turn, missing our opportunity to change the world.

There are many questions:

- How much do we (society and the government) really know about our local small businesses?
- How fast are they growing?
- How productive are they?

- How many are exporting?
- What is preventing their growth?
- Are they failing because they cannot scale?
- Is some growth necessary to thrive?

*What is preventing sole Proprietorships from growing?*

Research by the British Chambers of Commerce (BCC) has found that pension requirements, dismissal rules and sickness and absence rules are three of the biggest barriers preventing sole proprietorships from hiring their first employee and thus growing into small and medium sized businesses.

The Royal society for the encouragement of Arts, Manufacturing and Commerce (RSA) has made several recommendations to government to help encourage sole proprietorships to take on staff. These include; employee sharing, small business careers fairs for graduates and a suggestion that accountants should take over a wider business advice role.

Are these just the affects not the cause of the problem? Are these businesses unable to grow and scale because they are failing to solve a problem? They haven't established a big enough market for themselves to sustain their business. So the business owners are operating hand to mouth, applying bandages but not actually auditing their business to see whether it is really worth pursuing?

I strongly believe that it is not enough to support the creation of new businesses governments and the private sector should focus on lifting the productivity of existing firms and help them to scale.

So how do I do this on a company-by-company basis? Take a look at my blog on my website www.routesandbranches.com/blog and visit my YouTube channel to read and watch some of the ways Routes and Branches has helped UK businesses become more productive and scale.

How does this affect you my reader? Let's start from the viewpoint that not every business should scale. After all I are striving to create thriving rather than growing businesses and that means that some won't survive. Before attempting to scale every business first measure it to ensure it is performing well against some core criteria:

- Is it solving a big enough problem to warrant survival
- Would the people involved in the business thrive more, or better if they were contributing to an alternative organisation?
- Assuming the organisation is tackling a problem worth solving, is the problem neglected enough to leave them with enough potential market share to make their efforts worthwhile?
- Is the problem solvable?
- Will they get to a point where their business can thrive?

These are the measures I believe you should assess your own business against. Only when you meet these criteria are you able to scale in order to thrive.

If you determine that your business is worth scaling then adopting an international approach can help you. I will talk more about this later in the book, for now let's look at challenge 4.

## Challenge 4: Failure to plan

Exporting is an exciting and dynamic activity, which if undertaken professionally, can reap rewards for both the exporting company as well as the eventual overseas customers (Marketing Consultancy Division). Yet many businesses fail because they fail to prepare for future success. Instead they live by day-to-day, being carried along by the tide of wins and losses, hoping that things will turn out all right.

Many of the businesses I visit get very overexcited by an out of the blue overseas enquiry and with very little or in some cases no market research, plunge themselves into export only to face difficulties down the line. They are reactive opportunist exporters rather than strategic ones. I've come into businesses to help them problem solve at the point where they have accepted an order knowing nothing about the market or how to fulfil it and then getting bogged down in legislative requirements and logistics. It has been my role to sort out this order and then work with them to develop a strategic exporting plan so that they know where and why they are exporting to certain markets and how to benefit from overseas opportunities.

Strategic or purposeful exporters have two traits in common. They are committed to their export vision and they have a plan as to how they will achieve it.

Export success can be achieved by having good products to sell at a reasonable price, an organisational structure that optimises corporate and staff performance, and an awareness of the exporting rules, and regulations and any trade barriers in each of the targeted export countries.

## Challenge 5: Brexit

In the referendum on 23rd June 2016, the British people voted to leave the European Union. Theresa May the British Prime Minister invoked Article 50 on the 29th March 2017 and it began the United Kingdoms withdrawal from the European Union. The United Kingdom will leave the European Union on the 29th March 2019 and begin to chart a new course in the world.

I am going to assume that you are aware of article 50 and understand what the European Union is. If you need a quick recap you can take a look at my glossary.

The conservative government has introduced the European Union (withdrawal bill) to parliament. If passed it will end the primacy of EU law in the UK. This "Great Repeal Bill", as it was originally called, is supposed to incorporate all EU legislation into UK law in one lump, after which the government will decide over a period of time which parts to keep, change or remove.

Unpicking 43 years of treaties and agreements covering thousands of different subjects was never going to be a straightforward task. It is further complicated by the fact that it has never been done before.

The post-Brexit trade deal is likely to be the most complex part of the negotiation because it needs the unanimous approval of more than 30 national and regional parliaments across Europe, some of which may want to hold referendums.

As the UK Government negotiate our exit from the European Union, Great Britain has a once in a lifetime opportunity to build a stronger, fairer and more prosperous United Kingdom that is more open and outward- looking than ever before. For the first time in over 40 years, the UK will have its own independent trade policy (UK Government ).

*What happens next?*

In the White Paper "The Future Relationship between the United Kingdom and the European Union" published July 2018 the Prime Minister sets out the principles in which Brexit negotiations will continue.   The proposal underpins the vision set out by Prime Minister Theresa May at Lancaster House, In Florence, at Mansion House and in Munich. It addresses the questions raised by the EU and explains how the new relationship would work.   What benefits it would deliver to both sides and how it would respect the sovereignty of the UK as well as the autonomy of the EU.

Theresa May reasserts the vision that the UK is "an outward facing, trading nation; we (the UK) have a dynamic, innovative economy; and we live by common values of openness, the rule of law        and        tolerance        of        others". (www.gov.uk/government/publications, 2018)

The white paper sets out the UK's proposal for a principled and practical Brexit. On the basis of this proposal the UK's negotiating team will engage with the EU's at pace. This means finalising the Withdrawal Agreement and The Framework for the Future relationship.

Once the UK and the EU have reached agreement on the Withdrawal Agreement and the Future Framework, there will be a debate in both Houses of Parliament.  If the House of Commons support a resolution to approve the Withdrawal Agreement and the Future Framework, the Government will bring forward the Withdrawal Agreement and Implementation Bill to give the Withdrawal Agreement legal effect in the UK. In the EU, the

European Parliament must give its consent to the conclusion of the Withdrawal Agreement. The UK and the EU have a shared ambition to agree both documents by October in order to give sufficient time for their respective Parliaments to give their approval before the UK leaves the EU on 29 March 2019.⁅SEP⁆

*What does a principled and practical Brexit mean?*

A principled Brexit respects the UK public's decision to take back control of the UK's laws, borders and money. The UK Government anticipates that Brexit will influence five key areas of UK national life:

1. The economy.

2. Communities.

3. The Union.

4. Democracy.

5. The UK's place in the World.

For the purpose of this book, I focus on number five.

*What impact does Brexit have on Exporters?*

At this stage, there are still a huge number of ifs, buts and maybes in any assessment on the impact of Brexit on British exporters. The government's aspiration is to leave the Single Market but to secure the best possible deal for British business with regard to a free trade agreement with the European Union. Their aim is to continue to promote innovation and new ideas. To assert a fully independent foreign policy. But also to work alongside the EU to promote and protect shared values of democracy openness, and liberty.

In reality what are the areas British Business owners should be working on?

The procedures of trade with EU countries will change to be similar to trading with the rest of the world. Exporters will need to familiarise themselves with the requirements of UK customs relating to export clearance as well as the import clearance rules of the receiving country.

Another area is planning for currency volatility. In a study by Western Union Business Solutions (WUBS) 44% of respondents said that currency volatility is one of their biggest barriers to international trade yet 75% don't effectively plan for it. One of the things business owners can start to do is plan for currency volatility. There are a number of companies that can help with forex planning and we can make introductions to them for you.

Compliance is another area that SME's will need to track and study closely. I discuss this further below.

*Many UK SME's are frozen like rabbits in the headlights*

Anastassia Beliakova, head of trade policy at the British Chamber of Commerce (BCC), said that "almost half of our members have said that they don't take any steps at all to prepare [for Brexit]". She said that the BCC was trying to encourage its members to be "more proactive". (newstatesman.com)

The BCC has produced a "Brexit check-list" designed to help SMEs to compartmentalise their costs. I encourage you to take a look at this checklist.

Paul Uppal the small business commissioner at the Department for Business, Energy and Industrial Strategy (BEIS) drew inspiration from India. "From my experience, businesses are increasingly trying to take matters into their own hands, and forge partnerships that they themselves have control over [rather than as part of a bloc]. Consider the Access India programme, where the government identified British businesses that could directly collaborate with their companies. You don't need someone else to draw up the terms for you."

*What was the single market?*

The development of the Single Market has created a unique system where goods, services, capital and people can move freely across 28 countries. For exporters, this has removed a considerable amount of control over the movement of goods between EU countries, at the cost of significant changes, often drastic, in legal standards for products, technology, employment, legal process and environmental control. The benefit for many exporting companies is that they can send and receive goods with much greater ease and speed than ever before. The harmonisation of standards has also made it less complicated to introduce products into new EU markets, because where a common or harmonised standard exists, the rules in the target country usually accord with those the exporter is already following.

### So what impact will leaving the Single Market have?

Brexit will see the UK leave the Single market and Customs Union. The UK Governments vision when designing a new trading relationship is to ensure frictionless access at the border to each other's markets for goods.   The government proposes the establishment of a free trade area for goods.  This free trade area would protect the uniquely integrated supply chains and "just-in-time" processes that have developed over the past 40 years.  It would also avoid the need for customs and regulatory checks at the border, and mean that businesses would not need to complete costly customs declarations.  It would also enable products to only undergo one set of approvals and authorizations in either market before being sold in both.

The White paper "The Future Relationship between the United Kingdom and the European Union" splits the Brexit negotiations into 4 core areas as follows:

- Economic partnership.
- Security partnership.
- Cross-cutting cooperation.
- Institutional arrangements.

Each will have a knock on effect on exporters.

### So what are the components of the economic vision?

1. A common rule book.

2. Continued participation in EU organisations that provide authorizations for goods.

3. A facilitated customs arrangement.

4. No tariffs on any goods.

5. New arrangements for services and digital.

6. New economic and regulatory arrangements for financial services.

7. Continued cooperation on energy and transport.

8. Control of UK borders.

9. An open and fair trading environment.

*What are the components of the security vision?*

1. Continued cooperation.

2. A new security partnership.

3. Maintain existing operational capabilities.

4. Participation in key agencies.

5. Coordination on foreign policy, defence and development.

6. Wider cooperation in areas such as counter terrorism.

*What are the components of the cooperation vision?*

1. Protection of personal data.

2. Establish cooperative accords for science and innovation, culture and education, development and international action, defence research and development.

3. Fishing.

*Not let's take a look at the Institutional arrangements*

1. Association agreement.

2. Regular dialogue between leaders.

3. Resolution of disputes.

Every trading relationship has varying levels of market access, depending on the respective interests of the countries involved. The UK and EU are now working to develop a tailored approach to their trading relationship. The UK recognises that it cannot have all the benefits of the single market without its obligations. The UK proposes the establishment of a free trade area and a common rulebook for goods. The common rulebook would be legislated for in the UK by the UK Parliament and devolved legislatures. The UK seeks to participate in EU agencies that facilitate goods being placed on the EU market.

The UK has proposed new arrangements for financial services that preserve the mutual benefits of integrated markets and protect financial stability. But these would not replicate the EU's passporting regimes. Brexit will mean an end to free movement of people. The UK will have its own independent trade policy and represent itself at the World Trade Organisation (WTO.)

*Compliance*

When Brexit comes into force the biggest issue for many exporting companies is likely to be compliance. At present, product and technical standards are largely harmonised between EU countries, meaning that a product that is legal in the UK is usually (although not always) legal in other countries too. It also helps that evidence required to prove compliance in the UK is also accepted in other EU countries. Initially, it is likely that work will have been done to harmonize standards meaning that there should not usually be any need to an exporting company to adapt. However, over time both the UK and EU authorities are certain to alter their rules and to introduce new ones. A company that exports to other EU countries will need to keep up to date with changing rules in Westminster and Brussels.

The UK's proposal as set out in the White paper to parliament "The future relationship between the United Kingdom and the European Union" July 2018 covers compliance activity. The UK believes that manufactures should only need to undergo one series of tests in either market in order to be compliant in both. They, therefore propose the following compliance measures:

- Product testing.
- Labels and marks.
- Accredited assessment bodies.
- Standard manufacturing and quality assurance processes.
- Consistent rules for "responsible persons".
- Bespoke provisions for medicines.
- Standardised export licences.

The UK is seeking participation in the European Medicines Agency (EMA) The European Chemicals Agency (ECHA) and the European Aviation Safety Agency (EASA). This is with the aim of products only going through one approval mechanism.

To ensure that there is no market disruption as the UK and the EU transition from the implementation period to this new free trade area, the UK proposes that all manufactured goods authorizations, approvals, certifications, and any agency activity is undertaken under EU law (for example, to register a chemical), completed before the end of the implementation period, should continue to be recognized as valid in both the UK and the EU.

*Isolation*

The United Kingdom is an important market for the EU, and vice versa. In 2017 the value of imports and exports between the EU stood at over £423 billion, with the UK reporting £95 billion in trade deficits of goods with the EU. While post-Brexit Britain will remain an important export market for the EU-27, its isolation in Europe and loss of preferential access to the bloc's trading partners could have dramatic consequences.

Big business - with a few exceptions - tended to be in favour of Britain staying in the EU because it makes it easier for them to move money, people and products around the world.

The UK has proposed the establishment of a free trade area for goods including agri-food. Together with the wider free trade area, the FCA would preserve frictionless trade for the majority of UK goods trade, and reduce frictions for UK exporters and importers. The UK's goal is to facilitate the greatest possible trade, whether with the EU or the rest of the world.

## *Tariffs*

As long as Britain has been in the EU there hasn't being a need to talk about tariffs. That's because all trade within the European Economic Area is tariff-free. On top of that, the EU has trade agreements with 52 other countries as well.

After Brexit, Britain is going to have to negotiate new deals all on its own. That's both a problem and an opportunity.

A government, to raise the price of a product been imported into their country uses a tariff, sometimes called a tax or duty. For example you can use tariffs against foreign imports to protect businesses you care about, as the EU does with agricultural produce, but you do then run the risk of retaliation from your trading partners. A quota is another variation to be aware of. Rather than adding an extra tax onto a product, a government will limit the amount that can be imported.

The key body in all of this is the World Trade Organisation and at the moment the UK is only a member via its membership of the EU. The UK will automatically become a member in its own right as soon as it leaves the EU.

The principle of non-discrimination means that WTO members must not treat any member less advantageously than any other. In practice, this should prevent the EU introducing tariffs on the UK, which would discriminate against us, or the UK introducing similar tariffs on the EU.

The UK has proposed the phased introduction of a new Facilitated Customs Arrangement that would remove the need for customs checks and controls between the UK and the EU as if they were a combined customs territory, which would enable the UK to control its own tariffs for trade with the rest of the world. It would also ensure businesses paid the right or no tariff.

In combination with no tariffs on any goods, these arrangements would avoid any new friction at the border, and protect the integrated supply chains that span the UK and the EU, safeguarding the jobs and livelihoods they support.

Fortunately, protectionism is declining across the world as a result of the work of the World Trade Organisation. But it is still important to do market research to determine if your industry is involved in any trade disputes, or if there are any tariffs or quotas that you need to factor into your planning process.

### New Trade deals

Many countries have already expressed an eagerness to create new trade deals with the UK once it is separated from the EU, including Australia, the US and South Africa.

However, this all takes time. What is in the shops today was not ordered and made yesterday. From China, for example, the lead-time can be as much as 6 months. Equally, what is for sale in China and made by us could have been ordered 6 months ago. So, today's imports and exports are much more reflective of demand at the exchange rate of some time ago. A useful rule of thumb here--and no more than that--is that it takes some 18 months to 2 years for trade to fully reflect changes in exchange rates.

As the UK leaves the EU the government is committed to ensuring that the UK and EU businesses can continue to trade with one another. The UK also hopes to boost its trade relationships with old friends and new allies.

The UK's exit from the EU will provide considerable additional opportunities for UK business through potentially ambitious new trade arrangements and meaningful trade deals that play to the strengths of the UK economy. [SEP]

## What should I be doing now?

The majority of businesses operating with or in the UK should have already begun (Dechert):

- Reviewing and identifying aspects of the business that rely on, or assume the applicability of, pan-EU arrangements such as EU rules of origin and customs procedures, passporting for financial services, EU-wide medicine licenses, etc.

- Understanding the actual (or likely) position of the UK, the EU Governments and EU institutions on the contents of the exit agreement, as well as the ambitions for the future UK-EU trading relationship.
- Establishing what the UK's baseline obligations in the WTO and other international bodies means for your business.
- Identifying EU laws which currently impact both your operations and that of your wider industry.
- Identifying the nature and extent of interaction with pan-EU agencies.
- Considering a government relations strategy (whether directly or through an industry group). Identify key proposals or considerations. Make these reasoned, evidence-based, granular and ambitious, while taking account of political realities. Respond to government consultations.
- Considering the impact on your supply chains and customer base.
- Looking at the nuts and bolts of your business including your data protection obligations; contractual terms; employment rights; intellectual property plans; and ongoing litigation.

# Section 3: My seven steps to export success

In the introduction, I said that I aimed to challenge 99% of UK businesses to export. In this section, I will provide you with tools and resources to help you to do so. Some of you may have jumped straight to this section. If so use the practical resources it applies but then go back to read the context of my advice especially as you get to step seven thrive. Brexit beating thriving businesses will need to be sustainable and that will mean changing our economic and leadership approach.

So what are my seven steps?

1. Values
2. Vision
3. Fear
4. Power
5. Authority
6. Legitimacy
7. Thrive

Values, Vision and fear are foundation modules for any successful business whether or not it exports. To grow and thrive it's really important to get these right. I could write a book on each of them alone, so by no means have I covered everything in my chapters. What I have done is situate their importance in the context of export. If you want to learn more about these points I've added videos and podcasts to my website which elaborate further.

Power, Authority and Legitimacy are the key export skills steps as they encourage you to develop your brand, position it correctly and legitimise it across multiple markets. I show you how to create a thriving international brand. How to identify and address relevant compliance issues and how to win customers in the market.

Finally, step seven Thrive is about creating more than business success it's about creating a business that is successful within the boundaries of Kate Raworths doughnut economics.

You can download my seven steps to export success checklist on my website where you will also find a link to the "Routes" course which is a practical course to guide you through each step and help you to apply the principles to your business.

# Step 1: Values

I'm often asked what is the key to building a successful international business? The key to export success is learning to prioritize effectively. Choosing what matters to you and what does not matter to you is based on your finely tuned values.

Most companies need to develop a strategy that enables their business to thrive. What do I mean by thrive? To thrive is to "prosper" and "flourish". In other words to "grow or develop in a healthy or vigorous way, especially as the result of a particularly congenial environment"

Business values are really crucial part of any thriving business. It's the motivation for what you do, how you do it, how you're going to be interpreted by your customers, how you work with your supply chain, and how you influence those that back your business and finance it. Finding something important and meaningful to your business is the most productive use of your time and energy.

When you're running your own business, you are in control. You decide what you work on. You have the opportunity to create a business that is as you want it to be – a venture that truly reflects your own enthusiasm, passion and values.

The right strategy is one that enables the business owner to delegate whilst safe in the knowledge that their employees are acting in a consistent and responsible way. They key to consistency is sharing core values.

Many people think that values are ethics or morals; they're not. Values are what is important to us, what we hold dear to us, and what gives us purpose. The things that you believe are important in the way you live and work. These are your priorities and the measures you use to determine if life or your business is turning out the way you wanted it to. Your measures determine whether or not you are thriving or failing.

Values reflect who we are on a daily basis, in everything we do at home and at work. When your values are been met by the events in your life you tend to be happy and contented. When things don't align with your personal values you can become unhappy.

When you define your personal values, you discover what's truly important to you. When you define your business values, you discover what is truly important to your business.

So now we are going to look at some of the techniques I use with my clients to help them to define their values.

*What are the main benefits of values?*

Your values help you to measure whether or not you are thriving or failing. Beyond that values give you a sense of energy, motivation, and can help you with resourcefulness, particularly in times of challenge.

Values affect how you work, how you are received, and the interactions that you have with your customers, supply chain, and finances. They are fundamental to determining the type of business you are and the type of business you are perceived to be.

*So what are the benefits of understanding your values?*

By consciously stating and understanding your values you will have a greater sense of energy, commitment and enthusiasm for starting, developing and running a business. It will give you greater determination and resourcefulness helping you to overcome the inevitable challenges that go hand in hand with being a business owner.

*Your values will affect a number of areas:*

1.  How you work,

2.  How you wish your work to be received and

3.   How you interact with customers, suppliers and funders.

*When your values are misaligned:*

So what happens if you are unaware of what your values are, have not yet defined them or feel as though your business is not aligned?

You're probably experiencing some of the following:

- Stressed and a sense of being out of control.
- Conflict or are torn between the different facets of your business.
- Excessively busy with every minute crammed with stuff but feel like you're getting nowhere.
- Drained from constantly rushing to tick off your to do list that just keeps getting longer.
- Regretful about what you've done in the past.

Don't worry I can help you.  Which is why I have created the "Routes" course, which takes you through my seven steps and gives you practical ways to apply the information to your own business.

*Your definition of success*

Thinking about how you define success can help you to better understand your values.  Success is a very personal thing, what drives one person may be radically different for another. The same goes for business success.

Consider the following questions: Why do I consider this to be a success/failure? How am I choosing to measure my business? By what standards am I judging myself and everyone around me?

Top tip: Create a page in your journal to answer each of these questions.  Don't overthink it write what comes to mind.  You can go back to it later to work with what you have written to help you make changes to your business.

Our values determine the metrics by which we measure ourselves and everyone else.

They are the metrics that we use to determine if the changes we have made are positive or negative when we assess our impact on the world. I was asked by one of my early readers if I thought that "values" was too foundational for this book. I think the opposite; values are fundamental. I would liken them to breathing. We take breathing for granted but mastering your breathing is one of the most powerful things you can do manage yourself and manage your impact on the world. The same is true for our values. We can have "shitty" (Manson M. ) values that do not serve us. Or we can take time to master our values and understand the mechanism they become for driving our impact on the world.

When Routes and Branches works with businesses looking to expand overseas, we initially look at what the business owner's definition of success is.

- In what direction do they want their business to grow?
- What impact will that bigger vision have on the whole of their business?
- And which values are aligned to that vision?

Once a business owner understands what values are aligned to their vision, they begin to embed those values in the whole of the business. They can then increase the impact of the business by communicating their values to others including their team and customers.

Top tip: Make a list of the ways that you would like your business to grow. Then consider whether or not this is aligned to your values.

*Embedding the core values into your work*

- One of the activities that I ask you to do in our "Routes" course is to identify your values from a list. Once you are aware of what your values are you can begin to examine them in relation to every aspect of your business. You should consider what impact your values have on;
- Your product or service

- Your brand, and marketing message
- Human resources
- Production
- Your supply chain
- Your strategic direction

Top tip: Consider your values and then analyse them in relation to each of these aspects.

Your brand values need to be entrenched into the whole business and understood by everybody that works for you. Values give your brand a sense of purpose. They enable your customer to relate to you and make your brand more appealing to certain groups and niches.

One of the ways that you can embed your core values into your work is to recognize people when they live the core values, especially in difficult situations – publicly and in person. When they don't, promptly and constructively coach them on how they could have handled the situation in a way that would have been consistent with the core values.

*Why it's important to measure performance and set targets against your values*

Measuring your business performance and setting targets are important processes for helping your business to thrive. Thriving businesses need to control their processes in order to;

- Expand the business and take on more staff
- Create new departments within the business
- Appoint new managers or directors
- Expand the business into new regions
- Expand the business internationally

One of the ways that business owners can measure the performance of the business is to conduct a strategic business review.

*What is a strategic business review and what does it have to do with business values?*

A strategic business review is an in depth examination of your business. The purpose of carrying out such an assessment is to assess the success of strategic or operational change in your business. When assessing strategic or operational change, your values can be used as a measure of success.

- Strategic business reviews are useful if:
- You are uncertain about how well your business is performing
- You want to know how to get the most out of your business or market opportunities
- Your business plan is out of date
- Your business is moving in a direction different to the one you had planned
- The business is becoming difficult or unresponsive to market demands
- You are preparing to expand into an overseas market

*Values and their impact on your export success*

It is very important that you understand the culture of your company and the things that matter most to you when expanding into new geographies.

Values are particularly important when trying to translate your business vision to customers overseas that might not necessarily understand the nuances of your business in the UK, but can often relate to a core value and thus find it easy to purchase from you.

Not everyone in the world values the same things you do. One big mistake company's make when entering new countries is assuming that what matters to them also matters to their potential customers around the world.

Cross-cultural awareness is really important when thinking about our values and exporting our business overseas. It's important to understand how people do business with one another in different cultures. Our values and our respect for cultural norms can really help us to integrate our business in other countries.

Travel is a fantastic self-development tool, because it extricates you from the values of your culture and shows you that another society can live with entirely different values and still function and not hate themselves. This exposure to different cultural values and metrics then forces you to re-examine what seems obvious in your own life and to consider that perhaps it's not necessarily the best way to live. (Manson, The Subtle Art of Not Giving a F*ck:)

### *Your Values can change over time*

Our values tend to be fairly stable. They don't have strict limits or boundaries. Instead they tend to act as a guidance to help you understand what is important to you and what is not. Overtime values can change as our life changes, or as our business changes. For example at the beginning of our career earning money might be our main priority but once we have had a family creating a better work life balance may become our priority. In our business launching our product might be our first priority but overtime we may want to make product adaptations to become more environmentally friendly.

In order to achieve sustainable success, companies must repeatedly re-examine their sense of purpose and values and make sure that they serve the organization well, and that the organisation is a true reflection of the values upon which it has being built.

In his book the Subtle art of not giving a fu*k Mark Manson argues that if you want to change how you see problems you have to change what you value and how you measure failure and success. He goes on to discuss the difference between "good values" and "bad values."

Good values are 1) reality-based, 2) socially constructive, and 3) immediate and controllable. Bad values are 1) superstitious, 2) socially destructive, and 3) not immediate or controllable (Manson).

- An authentic and inspiring purpose based on good values therefore allows for:
- A constant, consistent sense of focus
- A strong emotional engagement both within the company and with its customers and partners
- Continuous, pragmatic innovation

When a business has a clear vision, it's easier to create products and services of value.

## Brexit doesn't have to hold us back it could propel us forwards.

In chapter one, I eluded to the role Brexit is playing in helping the UK to re-establish itself. As part of this process as a nation we have entered into a conversation and debate about what our values are. When determining what we do and don't want from trading relationships with Europe and the rest of the world we have to understand and be able to articulate our values. Every decision we make and policy we change as a result of Brexit will be a reflection of what is important to us as a nation and what is not. As a nation we will have to live with the consequences of those decisions. Either way Brexit is an opportunity for us to position ourselves on the global stage and create the conditions necessary to thrive. Brexit will change the world.

# Step 2: Vision

In this chapter we will explore "vision". Both the UK's vision for a post Brexit economy and also your vision for your company. Let's begin with your company vision.

In the introduction I said all businesses have three things in common:

1. Something to sell,

2. Something has to solve a problem or be desirable to people so that they want to buy it,

3. And once they have bought it, it has to be so good that they want to recommend it to others.

I'd like to add a fourth. Successful exporters also have a clear vision of the world they want their business to be a part of. A vision of the world they want to live in as a business owner. It is in realising this vision that they achieve maximum impact for their businesses and change the world.

So number one. In order to have something to sell you must have a "vision" an idea about the problem you want to solve and an idea of how to solve it. Vision describes some achievement or future state that the organization wants to accomplish. A vision has to be shared in order to do what it is meant to do – which is inspire, clarify and focus the work.

You realize your vision by producing a product or service. You test the product or service in market to make sure that it really does solve the problem. Then you continue to adapt and improve on your solution until it's so good that the people that bought it are willing to buy more and recommend your solution to their family and friends.

It is quite common for Business owners to lose sight of their vision. When this happens it can have a detrimental effect on the business. Without being clear about where you are heading you can lose momentum, find it difficult to motivate your team and find it difficult to inspire your customers. Energy and business dwindles.

To export successfully you must be able to see your business as you want it to be in five or ten year's time. You must understand what you are trying to achieve and why. You must be able to communicate this why to others, (your team and your customers).

Knowing and being clear about where you're headed in business is something that must come from within. When you select your goals, you're more motivated to achieve them.     Belief and confidence in your business vision and your ability to make it happen is a state of mind that requires daily practice. Step by step, day-by-day your vision will become more powerful, detailed and clear and the journey to achieving it will become easier to navigate.

I encourage Routes and Branches customers to start with their biggest goal, the really scary, almost unrealistic audacious goal. If you start with this one it's easy to break it down into much smaller manageable pieces. If you start with something too easy it's often not inspiring enough to motivate the level of change you need in your business to be successful.

You need three things

1. Clarity about what you are trying to achieve. If you don't know what you want to happen you end up drifting aimlessly and not getting very far.

2. Confidence that what you are trying to achieve is possible. Our fears and doubts often cause us to lack confidence in our ideas.

3. Change, consistent actions to make your vision a reality

High-growth companies view global markets as an area of largely untapped opportunity that simply must be explored. They talk about global business as an investment in the future, a way to diversify and achieve scale for their business. Thriving businesses view export as an intrinsic part of their development and won't let anything stop them. Not even Brexit!

*How to achieve more clarity*

Are you in a quandary about how to meet your huge audacious goals? Do you feel stuck and don't know what to do next?

Make a quiet space to get clarity

Write down your objectives, goals, options and obstacles. Most people never do this, so if you do, this immediately gives you a competitive edge in this area.

Clear and concise goals and objectives are essential for an effective business plan. A goal should not be a broad concept. The goals should start with short-term objectives, which can be built upon for long-term success.

Ask yourself these questions:

- What does the best outcome look like?
    - For you the business owner
    - For your business
    - For your stakeholders
    - For your team

What are the possible solutions and options?

Remember that eliminating options is also a possibility and may be necessary to help you to achieve your main goals.

Be prepared to change direction. Remember the goals are only a guide. Do not be afraid to change the goals as your business moves forward. Goal setting should be viewed as a beginning point for achieving clarity in visioning the future of your business.

When the allotted time has passed, analyse the data. For example, did you achieve your 90 day goal? Why or why not?

Even with the best planning and intentions, some goals will not be reached. Businesses can run into unexpected challenges due to sudden changes in the economy or consumer trends. By going back to your detailed objectives, challenges can turn into new opportunities. The data will aid you in writing out a new business objective.

### So how do you make your vision tangible?

A great technique for nurturing your vision and purpose is to make your goals visual. Visualization is powerful because actions follow thoughts. Some people use vision boards; others opt for treasure maps. And still others set goals identifying specific dates for their achievement.

Vision boards also known as dream boards are one of the most valuable visualization tools available to you. The inspirational collages serve as your image of the future - a tangible example, idea or representation of where you are going. They should represent your dreams, your goals, and your ideal life. (Jack Canfield)

By representing your goals with pictures and images you will actually strengthen and stimulate your emotions because your mind responds strongly to visual stimulation. By putting a vision board somewhere you can see it every day, you will prompt yourself to visualize your ideal business on a regular basis. And that's important because visualization activates the creative powers of your subconscious mind and programs your brain to notice available resources that were always there but escaped your notice. (Jack Canfield)

Tip: decide what you want and write it down.

### How to communicate your vision to overseas clients

Once you are clear about your vision it is important to communicate it to your team. It's not good enough for senior leaders to develop a powerful vision. They need to make sure that the vision is clearly communicated to every employee, along with the goals that will help bring the vision to life. When people are clear on their destination, and are given a map to get there, as well as a tour guide communicating along the way, they will not only support the expedition, but usually will really enjoy the trip. Make sure that you meet with your team regularly to ensure that everyone remains on board and knows what direction you are heading in. Get in the habit of actively seeking employees' thoughts and opinions, especially prior to making decisions that impact their work. You'll experience fewer surprises along with greater employee engagement and productivity if you consistently encourage your employees to think and provide their input to help you and your team make the best decisions possible.

Read any vision statement and ask yourself, "Is that inspiring to the employees?"

*Communicate your vision to overseas clients*

The way that you discuss your businesses vision is just as important as the vision itself. Enthusiasm contributes to the increased impact of the message. You need to ensure that your customers and clients understand your vision. That means you must put together marketing collateral with clear and engaging messaging. Avoid dull, convoluted and 'corporate' communications – make it lively and interesting, but always professional. Use visual aids and updates to keep everyone aware of the progress you are making toward your vision.

*Different ways to communicate your vision*

How you communicate your brand to the masses can impact your effectiveness and determine if a customer recognizes your corporate message or chooses to ignore it.

- Use terms that are easily understood, unambiguous and as simple as possible.
- Make sure that your "deeper meaning" is well articulated and relevant to your employees.
- Communicate the vision through multiple channels

*How does your vision impact upon your market position?*

An aspirational vision and an ambitious strategy can help position your business for growth. The way that your business embodies its values and vision directly correlates to its market position as it impacts upon your consumers, community and the environment.

If you embody your values and vision correctly you can:

- Increase perception as a responsible business
- Generate potential new revenue streams
- Develop new business opportunities
- Gain exposure to new customers

*Position your business effectively*

It's vital that you position yourself in the market where you can stand out from your competitors, even if it is in relatively small ways. It could be in the manner you provide your service, or some other nice extras that your competitors don't offer. Also, are you selling a premium product aimed at the higher end of the market or something for the more budget-conscious? Maybe it's something in between. Being clear in your own mind helps you convey confidence and ensures a smoother path to success.

*Think strategically*

Identify your strengths and weaknesses, and use data to see what works and what doesn't. It's always a good idea to get honest feedback direct from clients so as to get an accurate picture of what you're doing well and what you need to improve on.

*Implementing your vision*

Developing a vision statement is not the end of the exercise. The hard work starts when you begin to implement your vision. A stated vision that is not implemented can have adverse effects. Your vision now needs to link to your strategic plan. In simplistic terms your vision establishes where you want to business to be. Your strategic plan determines how to get from where you are now to realising your vision. The first implementation process is to develop goals to help you to achieve your vision. The next step is to develop a series of actions to help you to reach those goals.

*An intangible vision for the future of the UK economy post Brexit is a Brexit frustration*

Currently there are two post Brexit visions in circulation. Theresa May's and The European Parliaments. Theresa May set out her vision in a speech at Mansion House on 2nd March 2018. Her vision is to "maintain the UK as a modern, open, outward looking, tolerant European democracy". In her speech Theresa May sets out 5 tests for the Brexit deal and says " As we leave the European Union, we will forge a bold new positive role for ourselves in the world, and we will make Britain a country that works not for a privileged few, but for every one of us"

Her five tests are as follows;

1. Implement the decision of the British people

2. The agreement must endure

3. Protect security and prosperity

4. Consistent with our values

5. Strengthen our union of nations and our union of people

The UK wants;

- The freedom to negotiate trade agreements with other countries around the world.
- To take back control of our laws.
- To create a frictionless border as possible between the EU and the UK so that we don't damage the integrated supply chains our industries depend on and we don't have a hard border between Ireland and Northern Ireland.

May identifies 5 foundations to underpin our trading relationship

1. Reciprocal binding commitments to ensure fair and open competition

2. An arbitration mechanism that is completely independent

3. Maintain an on-going dialogue

4. Arrangements for data protection

5.   Maintain links between people

The second vision was produced by the European Parliament in the form of a draft resolution titled "Motion for a resolution to wind up the debate on the framework of the future EU-UK relationship." This is a statement of the EU Parliaments priorities for the UK's exit. It proposes an "association agreement" between the EU and the UK. The Parliament does not have a formal role in the Brexit negotiations but it will have a binding vote on the eventual deal.

The EU vision indicates that The UK and the EU both want;

- Good access to each other's markets
- Competition between us to be fair and open
- To create a reliable and transparent means of verifying that we are meeting our commitments and resolving our disputes

Both visions leave some uncertainties:

- The extent to which it wants to diverge from European Single Market regulations, and in what sectors
- The UK must ensure that products only need to undergo one series of approvals in one country to show that they meet the required regulatory standards
- The UK will need to make a strong commitment that its regulatory standards will remain as high as the EU's.  That commitment in practice will mean that UK and EU regulatory standards will remain similar in future.

# Step 3: Fear

So you understand your values, and you have got a clear vision of the direction, which you are taking your business. So what's holding you back? In this chapter, I will identify some of the biggest fears holding business owners back and preventing them from exporting.

What happens when your something to sell comes to the end of its lifecycle? Or you start to run out of people to sell to? You no longer have something to sell that people want to buy. These are some of the questions I'm frequently asked.

I've distilled the others down into 6 core areas:

So what are the biggest fears?

1. Shrinking domestic market

2. Product Life cycle

3. Fear of missing out FOMO!

4. Fear of getting it wrong

5. Fear of the costs

6. Fear of being copied

## Accidental Exporter Syndrome

One two and three are the major cause of what I like to call "accidental exporter syndrome." A Syndrome is a group of symptoms, which consistently occur together, or a condition characterized by a set of associated symptoms. I've observed that accidental exporters tend to exhibit the same behaviours or make the same mistakes.

Let's look at the symptoms:

- Accidental exporters, export without a strategy. They stumble into it when they run out of other options or when they get an ad hoc enquiry out of the blue.

- Accidental exporters fear missing out and as a result are reactive. Their competitor starts to export so they think they had better export too.
- Accidental exporters export without a plan as a last resort, their home market is shrinking and they are not sure what else to do.
- Accidental exporters are fearful, unprepared and setting themselves up for further mishaps.
- Accidental exporters have abandoned their values or their vision or both.
- Accidental exporters are swept up in the excitement of an ad hoc enquiry
- Worst they have neglected their domestic business to the point that they feel export is the only option.

## What is exporting with purpose?

Are you looking to make your first export sale or expand into new foreign markets?

Exporting with purpose starts with;

- A clear vision of what you are trying to achieve.
- How you intend to achieve it?
- Who you intend to reach?
- What action you would like them to take?
- And by when would you like them to take this action?
- How frequently would you like them to take this action?

Top tip: explore each of these questions in turn and keep a record of your answers.

The key difference between accidental and purposeful exporting the intent. Purposeful exporters intend to create successful international businesses.

Successful purposeful exporting hinges on having a factual meaningful and efficient overseas business plan.

The plan should define the business, identify your goals and visions and provide measurable deliverables from which you can determine if you have been successful or not.

Purposeful exporters start by answering these key questions:

1. How will this new market fit into the companies growth plan?

2. Does the market have a need for the product or service?

3. Who is presently serving the market?

4. Does our product need to be modified?

5. What's the best route to market?

6. What resources will the business need to serve this market effectively?

Top tip: write your answers to each of these questions. Then a couple of days later go back through what you have written and make a note of your unknowns i.e. missing information that you need to research further. Then make a research plan/schedule so that you can start to gather the answers.

*So how do you develop a meaningful and efficient overseas business plan?*

You should begin with your vision statement to determine where you are heading then develop your strategic export plan from this vision. From your vision statement create a series of goals. Break down these goals into smaller action points. Your goals should be SMART.

Invest time in the market research phase it is fundamental to your success. Spending time here will prevent you from making costly mistakes elsewhere. Once you thoroughly understand your market you need to plan your finances. You should ask yourself how your export plan would impact upon your finances? Next, you need to plan operations, transport, sales and after-sales care. **Our Routes course is designed specifically for first-time exporters**

**and takes you through my Seven-step program to export success.**

## The 6 major export fears and how to overcome them

*A shrinking domestic market*

If you're in a marketing role within your organisation or you are the founder one of your responsibilities is to analyse and make recommendations as to where, when and how your company can grow. If you are only looking for opportunities in your own home country then you are limiting your opportunity to thrive.

The most obvious reason to export is to increase sales and earnings. But exporting can also help you to achieve economies of scale, greater purchasing strength, you can better utilise excess capacity, it can also help you to level seasonal fluctuations in sales. Looking at how people solve problems when they have limited resources can also be a great source of innovation.

Top tip: Watch Think Small to Solve Big Problems, with Stephen Dubner https://youtu.be/fypkPgeQxBQ

Exporters to emerging markets have created a new form of innovation; "Frugal innovation". Rather than stripping existing products of features, frugal innovation focuses on turning constraints into advantages (Thornton, 2012). There is often an extra benefit to inventing something that fills a basic need with extreme affordability: It can travel to other markets, including mature markets. You can find out more about frugal innovation in this you tube video https://youtu.be/DnQi7ndgx3Y

One of the biggest impacts that globalization has had on small businesses is the fact that every business with an Internet connection now has access to the global market. The Internet has changed the way we do business. Just about anything you want to purchase is available to buy around the clock across the globe. So what impact does this have on your ability to export? It almost certainly means that you have some global competition.

Are you seeing increasing requests from your customers to match prices from other websites? Are your customers beginning to negotiate harder and more often? Have you noticed more abandoned carts on your webpage? These are early indicators that your market place is shrinking.

A shrinking domestic market may be a real challenge for your business. Brexit coupled with lower consumer disposable incomes has caused uncertainty. Cautious consumers are saving rather than spending. This is shrinking the domestic market for many industries in the UK.

There are ways to purposefully overcome this challenge and grow your business. Small businesses that rely solely on their domestic market will experience restricted growth in the coming years and could fail due to market dilution. Offshore markets can offer the benefits of increased sales, the opportunity to achieve greater profit margins; an increase in revenue can fuel further growth.

Export success comes as a result of comprehensively following steps; don't try to take shortcuts. If your business is failing domestically it is unlikely to succeed overseas. Before trying to compete overseas you should take corrective action to improve your domestic business. I have developed a tool to test whether or not you are export ready. If you would like to begin your export journey you can also join our community and follow our routes exporting course.

*Product lifecycle*

All products pass through a sequence of stages known as their product lifecycle. Introduction, growth, maturity and decline. Each stage is associated with changes in the product's marketing position. You can use various marketing strategies in each stage to try to prolong the life cycle of your products. Over the typical life cycle total sales in the relevant market first increase at an increasing rate, then at a decreasing rate and finally decline.

*Product introduction strategies*

Marketing strategies used in introduction stages include:

- Rapid skimming - launching the product at high price and high promotional level.
- Slow skimming - launching the product at high price and low promotional level.
- Rapid penetration - launching the product at low price with significant promotion.
- Slow penetration - launching the product at a low price and minimal promotion.

During the introduction stage, you should aim to:

- Establish a clear brand identity.
- Connect with the right partners to promote your product.
- Set up consumer tests, or provide samples or trials to key target markets.
- Price the product or service as high as you believe you can sell it, and to reflect the quality level you are providing.

You could also try to limit the product or service to a specific type of consumer - being selective can boost demand.

*Product growth strategies*

Marketing strategies used in the growth stage mainly aim to increase profits. Some of the common strategies to try are:

- Improving product quality.
- Adding new product features or support services to grow your market share.
- Enter new markets segments.
- Keep pricing as high as is reasonable to keep demand and profits high.
- Increase distribution channels to cope with growing demand.
- Shifting marketing messages from product awareness to product preference.
- Skimming product prices if your profits are too low.

Growth stage is when you should see rapidly rising sales, profits and your market share. Your strategies should seek to maximise these opportunities.

Product maturity strategies

When your sales peak, your product will enter the maturity stage. This often means that your market will be saturated and you may find that you need to change your marketing tactics to prolong the life cycle of your product. Common strategies that can help during this stage fall under one of two categories:

- market modification - this includes entering new market segments, redefining target markets, winning over competitor's customers, converting non-users
- product modification - for example, adjusting or improving your product's features, quality, pricing and differentiating it from other products in the marking

*Product decline strategies*

During the end stages of your product, you will see declining sales and profits. This can be fuelled by changes in consumer preferences, technological advances and alternatives on the market. At this stage, you will have to decide what strategies to take. If you want to save money, you can:

- Reduce your promotional expenditure on the products.
- Reduce the number of distribution outlets that sell them.
- Implement price cuts to get the customers to buy the product.
- Find another use for the product.
- Maintain the product and wait for competitors to withdraw from the market first.
- Harvest the product or service before discontinuing it.

Another option is for your business to discontinue the product from your offering. You may choose to:

- Sell the brand to another business.

- Significantly reduce the price to get rid of all the inventory.

*How to market your product to maximise the product life cycle*

When marketing your product in a different country it is important to consider that your product may be at a different stage in its lifecycle in this overseas market than it is in your home market. As an exporter you need to identify where your product fits in the product life cycle and then leverage that stage to help you achieve maximum profit in your chosen market.

If your product is very innovative you will need to focus on market education. In overseas markets forget about national borders instead focus on amplifying your messages. Try to get publicity. Connect with industry thought leaders to try your product in exchange for a testimonial.

Now try to identify any industry clusters. Does the industry have an ecosystem of suppliers, producers and a locally trained workforce? Focusing on where an industry has several potential clients can save time and financial resources.

When you no longer have to explain what your product does you have established an early majority. This is the time to hire and train competent marketing and sales staff in the UK and in the overseas markets that you are targeting. Ideally you should hire bilingual staff. In this stage it is not uncommon to see new market entrants or even large industry players watching to see which technologies they would like to acquire from smaller companies. Make sure that you include a competitor analysis in your market research at this stage. You should also be identifying potential strategic partnerships. Partnerships that enhance your existing business can be a fantastic route to new markets at this stage. Partnering among global organizations—even among competitors—has become more commonplace as businesses encounter issues that are too large or complex to handle on their own (Deloitte, 2014). Businesses are also beginning to partner with NGO's and the public sector to deliver sustainable solutions. They are increasingly finding places where they can bring complementary knowledge, experience, and skills to bear on social problems.

Partnerships between companies and non-profits are beginning to result in new market opportunities. Operating in new markets or with new market segments can carry considerable risk, particularly where firms confront strong local brands, unfamiliar consumer preferences, and distribution challenges. Partnering with non-profits and foundations provides a way of sharing the risk; businesses benefit from the credibility of trusted non-profits and from access to local knowledge.

In the next stage the market is becoming saturated. New entrants are starting to develop products that superseded yours. At this stage customer service becomes critical and is where you should focus your time and resources. Production efficiencies are more critical as price pressures can squeeze profit margins.

In the final stage you should be developing or acquiring new products.

*Fear of Missing Out*

Fear of missing out is an apprehension that others may be having rewarding experiences that you are absent from. In business, this presents itself as "fear of missed opportunity" The term was coined in 2004 by Patrick J McGinnis in an article in a Harvard Business School magazine, The Harbus.

Exporting is an investment. "FOMO" is one of the biggest emotional traps in investing. Most long-term investors understand how important it is to set goals, remain focused on them, and ignore distractions.

When you are caught in a loop of FOMO you tune out of the real world and into the fake one. The key to overcoming FOMO is to refocus your attention. Stop paying attention to what you think others are doing and start focusing on what is really going on in your business. What good things are you taking for granted in your business? What steps could you take to help you achieve your vision?

Before you jump at a "once in a lifetime opportunity" to enter XYZ market it is important to lower the volume of emotion and tune in to evidence.

It's vital to assess your risk tolerance. If, after assessing your risk tolerance, you decide to explore the new market it is wise to educate yourself before investing. Do your market research. It is vital to understand the market and the consequences entering it will have on your whole business. Make sure that you are exporting with purpose and for the right reasons rather than bumbling into the unknown through fear of missing out. Our Routes course helps you to identify the fears that are holding back your business and shows you a number of successful strategies to overcome them.

*Fear of getting it wrong*

Having some fear of mistakes can be a good thing; it can help to improve your performance. But excessive fear causes problems.

Exporting can be a great opportunity to develop new customers and increase profits. However, trading internationally presents extra risks and challenges that you wouldn't necessarily face in your domestic market. You can't eliminate these risks altogether, but you can manage and minimise them. I am going to identify some of the risks associated with international trade and explore some of the ways you may overcome them.

You can group the major risks into three categories, political, financial and legal.

| Group 1 | Country political | Political risk implies that a government could interfere with export/commerce in some way. |
|---|---|---|
| Group 2 | Currency exchange Transfer Credit | Financial risks can be overcome by using payment methods with a level of security. |
| Group 3 | Non performance Transport Legal Risk of fraud | Different markets have different laws and regulations it is therefore imperative to obtain legal advice from a respected legal practitioner. |

Dealing with customers in other countries adds a layer of complexity to any trade deal. Knowing what risks are associated with exporting to each country helps you to determine how you might mitigate against each risk.

By adopting effective risk management techniques you can manage risk within your business. Effective risk management is a three-step process:

1. Risk identification

2. Risk assessment

3. Risk control

Market research helps you understand the risks of doing business in a particular country. You can then decide how you want to control those risks. Initial 'desk research' in the UK is a useful starting point. Don't be afraid to ask for support.

There is a number of professional organisations set up to support exporters, use them to help you. If you are unsure where to start or who to go to for help I would be happy to answer your questions.

You can email me directly [Jennifer@routesandbranches.com](mailto:Jennifer@routesandbranches.com)

*Get it right with my seven-step process*

Efficient planning is one of the most effective ways to avoid costly mistakes.

Here are my 7 steps for effective export planning:

1. Identify your exporting goal
2. Identify your export potential
3. Understand your competition
4. An international leadership
5. Understand your data
6. Find the right route to market
7. Draft your action plan

Not sure how to do this in practice? Sign up for our Routes course which takes you through this step by step and shows you how to apply the principles to your own business.

*Step 1: Identify your exporting goal*

When growing your business you should have a vision of your overall goal in mind. Your exporting vision should be linked to your overall vision for the growth and development of your company. Questions you may want to consider are:

- Do you intend to sell the business?
- Change your role?
- Expand it locally, nationally, internationally?

Many small business owners fail to make the progress they would like because they only have a vague idea of their end goal with no defined purpose or vision, which often means that they get stuck going round in circles.

It is vital that you have a clear vision so that you can select an appropriate business model and structure. Business models and structures are different to facilitate different business outcomes.

1.  What are the implications of your vision?

2.  How will your vision influence the way you structure your business?

### Step 2: Identify your export potential

Now dropping down a level from the business itself to your core product. What happens when your something to sell comes to the end of its lifecycle? Or you start to run out of people to sell to? You no longer have something to sell that people want to buy?

There is no doubt that for some companies exporting can prove a lifeline, but that rarely happens without a plan.

You need to understand where there is a market for your product. Consider which markets want your products? Will you need to make modifications or adaptations to enable your product to sell in your chosen market? Is it easy to get your goods to them? Are there any prohibitive import duties or taxes? Will you get paid easily?

There are several ways to evaluate the export potential of your products. The most basic approach is to examine the domestic sales of your products. If you are successful at home the next step is to determine why?

To determine demand first choose a market to examine. Analyse the market to discover the market conditions and whether it contains a significant number of potential clients.

Next you will need to consider the competitive advantages of your firm. Without a competitive advantage, your company can never be successful internationally since competitors can simply capture all your potential customers. This competitive advantage can change drastically from market to market and will largely depend on the positioning of your company.

Next perform a PESTLE analysis to understand the environmental, political and social factors that could influence your ability to do business in your chosen market.

Next you must determine if you have the resources necessary to export successfully.

### Step 3: Understand your competition

You also need to understand your competition. Who are they? Where do they sell? Where are they successful? (Chamber International, 2018)

Knowing who your competitors are, and what they are offering, can help you to make your products, services and marketing stand out. It will enable you to set your prices competitively and help you to respond to rival marketing campaigns with your own initiatives.

You can use this knowledge to create marketing strategies that take advantage of your competitors' weaknesses, and improve your own business performance. You can also assess any threats posed by both new entrants to your market and current competitors. This knowledge will help you to be realistic about how successful you can be.

You are much more likely to survive and thrive if you focus on markets that others have neglected.

### Step 4: An international leadership

Businesses lacking international perspective among their leaders are often timid about moving into new markets. A fear of the unknown is normal. Because they do not have first-hand experience, they sometimes fail to prioritize global expansion. They are not convinced that they need to diversify geographically in order to scale.

One of the keys to successful export, and possibly the most important, is having leadership buy in from the top down. Having leadership support helps drive the importance of export to the company. It also assists with accountability and establishing appropriate expectations.

It is not always easy to establish leadership buy in. Get to know your leaders so that you can determine the most appropriate way to approach them. Consider for example how they prefer to receive information. Review your numbers in advance. You need to be able to demonstrate how export will make or save the company money. Try to anticipate questions and concerns in advance and be prepared to address these concerns. Share your export plan and be able to discuss what the implementation process would involve. Be conscious of budgeting processes and business dependencies to make sure that your proposal is not conflicting.

### Step 5: Understand your data

Companies that struggle with international growth tend to have a hard time answering these basic questions:

- What are your top ten countries by revenue share?
- By customer base?
- What percentage of your marketing budget is allocated toward international?
- What percentage of your sales team?

Often, just the exercise of obtaining this data helps a company get a better understanding of their true international picture.

### Step 6: Find the right route to market

Your route to market is how you sell your product and how you plan your sales. It's one of the most important things to get right. You can have the most amazing product or service ever created but it will fail if it's not put in front of the right customers. To maximise your business success you need to focus on identifying the best route to market.

The first step in identifying the right route to market is to get to know your customer. You will need to ask your customers what they buy, where they buy, how they prefer to buy and why they buy. Whoever you are selling to - whether a consumer or a business customer - you will need to appreciate the needs of the individual buyer and ensure that you can cater to them. The success of every route-to-market strategy depends on the depth of understanding a business has of their customers, their needs, their expectations and their behaviours.

Once you understand your customer you can begin to consider which are the most appropriate sales channels or routes. There are pros and cons with all sales channels. You may be able to supply overseas customers directly from the UK. Or you might have to establish a local presence; whether that's through an agent, distributor, reseller or your own team. What's right for you will depend on what you are selling and the size of the market.

In summary, there are four options:

1. Sell directly

2. Use a distributor

3. Use an agent

4. Create a joint venture

Understanding the different distribution options in your new market is an essential first step to export success. It is important to understand where customers are going to buy your products. Once you understand the top distribution channels for your product, decide which channel is right for you.

You'll need to research and be able to answer the following questions;

- Do we (the business) want to enter a channel that is growing faster overall or growing faster for our product?
- Are we (the business owners) willing to give up more control for faster sales?
- Do we (the business owners) want to work with one or multiple partners?
- So you have decided on the right channel now you need to decide the right partner or partners;

- Does it make more sense for your company to work with an established player or an up and comer you can grow with?
- Does the partner have a presence in other channels that they could help you expand?
- Do you want to work with a local player that knows the market or a multinational that could have more resources at its disposal?

Developing trust with local partners is critical to getting your product into an unfamiliar market. You need to be discriminating when choosing an agent or distributor and you need to be persistent. Look who else they have on their books.

You need to make sure that your product and sales channel are well suited to one another;

- Your sales channel needs to be one that customers will actually use
- It needs to make economic sense
- Consider how complex your sales channel needs to be

Don't assume that your competitors have selected the correct sales channel. Do you market research and determine the best fit for your business.

Once you have decided on your route to market and sales channels you will need to inform and promote them to your customers. For this you will need a strategic, financial and marketing plan.

### Step 7: Draft your action plan

Know where you are going, how you'll get there, what it will cost you, and what profit you can make. Take a close look at your readiness or use our export readiness checklist available to download on our website. You should evaluate your strengths, weaknesses, opportunities and threats.

Make sure your operations are lean. If you need to improve productivity its best to do that before you begin exporting.

Your export plan should include:

- Your people
- Your capacity including financial
- Your packaging
- Your knowledge

There are two types of export plan. The keep it simple business plan sometimes called the "back of the napkin" business plan which is typically short and sweet. It simply explains what the business does, what the business owner wants to do export wise and how they intend to get there.

Alternatively, there is a traditional export plan, which tends to be split into the following sections:

- A profile of your current business
- An industry analysis
- Identify products with export potential
- Marketability: matching your products or services with a global trend or need
- Determine market expansion pros and cons
- Identify the markets to pursue
- Conduct an export market sales analysis
- Short and long term goals.

Your export plan will provide you with:

- A disciplined approach to enter the market
- An understanding of the environment in which you'll be working in terms of the competition, potential partners and the regulatory framework
- A competitive position from which to enter the market.
- A budget for your venture
- The stages of the expansion and insurance against risks
- An implementation schedule
- Details about who is responsible for each task

## *Fear of Cost*

Expanding your business into international markets can be very challenging. It costs money to do it right. Sometimes it takes years for you to achieve a return on investment. So why do it? Importing and exporting products enables business growth.

For some businesses the financial strain of exporting outweighs the benefits. Business owners have to make choices about the projects their business can afford to do, and that includes making the decision of whether or not to expand internationally.

## *So what are the costs associated with exporting?*

There are 9 major costs associated with exporting; I have listed them here for your reference;

1. Market research

2. Setting up local company offices

3. Overseas sales agents

4. Using a distributor

5. Packaging and labelling

6. Insurance

7. Taxes

8. Transportation

9. Chasing payment

## *Cost 1: Market research*

It can easily run to thousands of pounds to conduct extensive market research. As a result many small businesses don't internationalise. Or they internationalise without conducting any market research.

Market research doesn't have to be prohibitively expensive. Basic research can be done online. A market visit can provide invaluable insights.

Internationalization consultants like Routes and Branches provide deeper understanding of each market and culture and can provide you with a strategic exporting plan and the necessary support to implement it effectively.

## Cost 2: Setting up local offices

Setting up a local office may not necessarily be the right route to market for your business. Before entering a new market it is important to thoroughly analyse your route to market options to determine which are available to you and which are the most suitable for your business.

What are the routes to market?

- Direct selling
- Selling wholesale
- Distance selling
- Online selling
- Combination of channels

In order to determine the most appropriate route to market for your business you need to consider how and where your customers shop. You also need to consider how much it will cost and whether you have the resources and ability to manage this channel.

Exporting is a very expensive process, so to cut down costs think about whether you actually need to have a permanent presence in your chosen area. You may not necessarily need an office when you're starting out so think about a virtual office. This can give you an address and phone number without the maintenance costs that come with a physical office.[ii]

## Cost 3 and 4: Overseas sales agents or distributors

A sales agent acts on your behalf in the overseas market by introducing you to customers who you supply and invoice direct. They are paid a commission for any sales they make ranging between 2.5 per cent and 15 per cent. The key benefit of using an overseas sales agent is that you get the advantage of their extensive knowledge of the target market. You need to make sure that you have accounted for the sales commission when pricing your product or service for the overseas market.

A distributor **buys your goods** from you and then takes full responsibility for selling them on in the overseas market. While the role of a sales agent is to find you customers, a distributor is your customer. However, it is likely that in order to attract an overseas distributor you would need to sell your products to them at a more competitive price so that they have some profit margin when reselling into the market. Make sure that you price properly so as to get the balance right between attracting a distributor and making a profit. Exporting shouldn't be loss making.

Bonus: Learn how to get the most out of your overseas partners https://routesandbranches.com/getting-international-expansion-partner/

*Cost 5: Packaging and labelling*

Proper packaging and labelling not only makes the final product look attractive but also save a huge amount of money by saving the product from wrong handling the export process.

Labelling on product provides the following important information:

- Shipper's mark
- Country of origin
- Weight marking (in pounds and in kilograms)
- Number of packages and size of cases (in inches and centimeters)
- Handling marks (international pictorial symbols)
- Cautionary markings, such as "This Side Up."
- Port of entry
- Labels for hazardous materials

Different countries have different packaging and labelling requirements. Before you begin exporting it is important to research the packaging and labelling requirements so that you can make product adjustments to meet the need of your export market. If you intend to export to multiple markets it would be advisable to create a comparison table detailing the different product labelling and packaging requirements for each market. This sounds like a lot of work but will save you lots of money by avoiding mistakes. Routes and Branches can assist you to develop this tool for your business.

### Cost 6: Export Insurance

Trade credit insurance, business credit insurance, export credit insurance, or credit insurance is an insurance policy and a risk management product offered by private insurance companies and governmental export credit agencies to business entities wishing to protect their accounts receivable from loss due to credit risks such as protracted default, insolvency or bankruptcy. Trade credit insurance can include a component of political risk insurance, which is offered by the same insurers to insure the risk of non-payment by foreign buyers due to currency issues, political unrest, expropriation etc. Trade credit insurance is purchased by business entities to insure their accounts receivable from loss due to the insolvency of the debtors. The product is not available to individuals. The cost (premium) for this is usually charged monthly, and are calculated as a percentage of sales for that month or as a percentage of all outstanding receivables.

### Cost 7: Taxes

Import duty is a tax collected on imports and some exports by a country's customs authorities. It is usually based on the imported good's value. Depending on the context, import duty may also be referred to as customs duty, tariff, import tax or import tariff. It is important to research the taxes in advance of exporting and also familiarise yourself with who is responsible for payment.

### Cost 8: Transport

Shipments are categorised into two broad categories, bulk shipment and small shipment. Bulk shipment can then be categorised into liquid bulk and dry bulk. To cater for the movement of these shipments, shipping companies provide two types of service tramp and liner. Tramp shipping provides service on demand and carries bulk between nominated ports. Liner shipping provides a scheduled service to advertised ports. Liner shipping receives the shipment, irrespective of characteristics, volume, weight and quality of cargo. Freight rates are fixed and made known to traders in advance. Prices are often quoted on a CIF basis or as per Incoterm 2000.

- The major costs included are:
- Labour charges for handling
- Road transport charges
- ICD charges
- CFS charges
- Port terminal handling charges
- Clearing charges
- Consolidation charges
- Liner freight
- On carriage charges payable at the destination port
- Transport insurance
- Duties and taxes
- Storage and demurrage charges

### Cost 9: Chasing payment

Widespread late payment has lead to British SMEs facing a collective £40 billion shortfall as they wait for their customers to cough up. (www.londonandzurich.co.uk) SMEs can be forced to wait long periods to receive late payments, leaving them without the cash flow to pay their suppliers and providers. This creates a knock-on effect that only worsens the situation.

Costs include:

- Working hours spent chasing late payments
- Interest on payments missed due to late payments
- Admin fees
- The adverse effect on your credit rating caused by missing payments as a result of late payments

- Making use of overdraft facilities, credit cards etc.

Chasing outstanding overseas payments can be even more costly to businesses so make sure that you understand your rights and use the export finance mechanisms available to you to help you to mitigate risks associated with late payment.

## *What determines a successful export pricing strategy?*

Pricing your product properly, giving complete and accurate quotations, choosing the terms of the sale, and selecting the payment method are four critical elements in making a profit on your export sales.

It is likely that when you begin selling your products in other markets that you will have a different pricing structure to the one you use in the UK.

To develop an appropriate pricing strategy you need to research your target markets. Consider the prices your competitors are charging. Investigate the cost of compliance with regulation and legislation. You may also have to make alterations to your product to make sure that it is appropriate for the market. You may also need to make changes to your packaging.

The key elements include assessing:

1. Your company's foreign market objectives,

2. Product-related costs,

3. Market demand, and competition.

4. Transportation,

5. Taxes and duties,

6. Sales commissions,

7. Insurance,

8. And financing.

Your companies market research should include an evaluation of all variables that affect the price range of your product or service.

Additional costs typically borne by the importer include;

- Tariffs
- Custom fees
- Currency fluctuation
- Transaction costs
- VAT

Pricing considerations

- What type of market positioning does your company want to convey from its pricing structure?
- Does the export price reflect your products quality
- Is the price competitive
- What type of discount should/could you offer to your foreign customers
- Should prices differ by market
- What pricing options are available if company costs increase decrease
- Is the foreign government going to view your prices as reasonable or exploitative?

Costs

The actual costs of producing a product and bringing it to market is key to determining if exporting is financially viable

**Cost plus pricing** is a **cost**-based **method** for setting the prices of goods and services. Under this approach, you add together the direct material **cost**, direct labour **cost**, and overhead **costs** for a product, and add to it a mark-up percentage (to create a profit margin) in order to derive the price of the product

**Marginal pricing** is when a business sells a product at a **price** that covers its manufacturing **costs** but not its overhead. The benefit of **marginal pricing** is that the lower **price** point increases customer demand. ... Small businesses can use this practice for a short-term revenue boost.

Other costs

- Fees for market research
- Credit checks
- Business travel expenses
- International postage/ telephone
- Translation
- Training
- Consultants
- Freight forwarding
- Product modification

*How does the weak pound benefit exporters?*

Exporters who sell their goods abroad benefit from a weaker pound. What the weak pound does is help British exporters sell their goods cheaper and this benefits foreign buyers who are getting more products and therefore more profit from their purchase. This ensures that British products - which tend to be much higher value than comparative foreign products are more competitive.

*Fear of IP infringement*

Intellectual property (IP) rights play an essential part in encouraging the universal benefits of innovation and creativity, as well as protecting the reputation of products and services and helping prevent consumers from being misled about the quality or provenance of goods. The high quality service offered by the UK's rights-granting bodies and courts system help to make the UK one of the best places in the world to protect and enforce IP rights (Taylor Wessing, 2018).

Intellectual property (IP) refers to a broad collection of rights relating to works of authorship, which are protected under copyright law; inventions, which are protected under patent law; marks, which are protected by trademark law; and designs and trade secrets.

*What are the real risks?*

- You are sued in an attempt to put you out of business

- A larger competitor completely ignores your IP
- You don't have the funds to recover from one and two
- You are sued by a non-producing entity
- A third party challenges your IP patent in an IPR
- You need more development money but don't want to give up control and can't get a loan

### How to protect your Intellectual Property when exporting

Many UK businesses, particularly small and medium-sized exporters, do not realize that their IP—copyrights, patents and trademarks—are not protected abroad.

Businesses should take steps to protect their IP both in the United Kingdom and in each country where they plan to do business.

Having the right type of intellectual property protection helps you to stop people stealing or copying:

- The names of your products or brands.
- Your inventions.
- The design or look of your products.
- Things you write, make or produce.

### Owning intellectual property

You own intellectual property if you:

- Created it.
- Bought intellectual property rights from the creator or a previous owner.
- Have a brand that could be a trade mark, e.g. a well-known product name.

Intellectual property can:

- Have more than one owner.
- Belong to people or businesses.
- Be sold or transferred.

*Considerations for International IP Protection*

National intellectual property laws create, confirm, or regulate a property right without which others could use or copy a trade secret, an expression, a design, or a product or its mark and packaging.

There is no such thing as an international patent, trademark or copyright. Copyright protection depends on national laws, but registration is typically not required. There is no real shortcut to worldwide protection of intellectual property.

*The impact of Brexit*

The UK system for protecting trademark rights is not affected by the decision to leave the EU. While the UK remains a full member of the EU then EU Trade Marks (EUTM) continue to be valid in the UK. When the UK leaves the EU, an EUTM will continue to be valid in the remaining EU member states.

When the UK has left the EU, UK businesses will still be able to register an EU trade mark, which will cover all remaining EU Member States.

In addition, the UK is a member of the international trade mark system called the Madrid System. This allows users to file one application, in one language, and pay one set of fees to protect trademarks in up to one hundred and thirteen territories including the EU.

When the UK leaves the EU it will need to establish its own Geographical Indications (GI) scheme with the WTO. GI's recognise the heritage and provenance of products which have a strong tradition or cultural connection to a particular place. Significant GI-protected products from the UK include Scotch whisky, Scottish farmed salmon, and Welsh beef and lamb. ⟦⟧

*Registered Community Designs (RCD)*

While the UK remains a full member of the EU, Registered Community Designs (RCD) continue to be valid in the UK. When the UK leaves the EU, an RCD will cover the remaining EU member states.

## The Hague System

The government has ratified the Hague Agreement and has joined this international system in a national capacity. The Hague System for the International Registration of Industrial Designs allows for registration of up to one hundred designs in over sixty six territories through filing one single international application.

## European patents

The UK's exit from the EU will not affect the current European patent system, which is governed by the (non-EU) European Patent Convention.

UK businesses can continue to apply to the European Patent Office for patent protection, which will include the UK. Existing European patents covering the UK are also unaffected.

The UK has ratified the Unified Patent Court Agreement and intends to explore staying in the Court and unitary patent system after the UK leaves the EU.

# Step 4: Power

In this chapter, I will explore the role that power plays in exporting. The impact that Brexit has had on the power of brand Britain. Then I will discuss the ways which you can leverage your power to maximise your export success. . In my experience understanding how to leverage your brand power and the power of brand Britain is one of the key distinguishing factors between successful and unsuccessful exporters.

## What is power?

Power is the ability or capacity to do something or act in a particular way. With power comes responsibility. Power is the ability to make things happen. When business owners exercise responsibility we attempt to answer the question: In whose interest is the power being used?

These two concepts are the yin and yang of our behaviour; they are how we balance our relations with ourselves with the interests of others.

Our sense of responsibility is inextricably linked to our values. Power makes things happen, but it is the exercise of an appropriate balance between power and responsibility that helps ensure that as many 'good' things happen as possible. (wabccoaches)

Our values often lead us to make judgements and these judgements have led us to associate responsibility and fault two concepts that often appear together in our culture. But they are not the same thing. Fault is past tense. Responsibility is present tense. Fault results from choices that have already been made. Responsibility results from the choices you're currently making, every second of every day (Manson, The Subtle Art of Not Giving a F*ck: A Counterintuitive Approach to Living a Good Life ).

So why have I drawn your attention to the concepts, power, responsibility and fault? In the context of Brexit it would be very easy for business owners to bury their heads in the sand feeling powerless and overlooked.  To blame the government for downturns in their business success and to use Brexit as a scape goat. It would be very easy for business owners to assume that they already know what is going to happen. To assume how the Brexit story ends. But assumed certainty is the enemy of growth. Nothing is for certain until it has already happened.

So let's take a look at power in the context of brand.

## What is a Brand?

Brand often means different things to different people. Many mistakenly see brand as the logo and ad campaign or what's on product packaging. They don't understand the strategic power that a fully articulated brand holds.

Brand is the impression people have of a product or service and is based on the sum of their experiences and interactions with it. Everything a brand does matters.

A brand should have a clearly defined set of values that guide how it behaves.

Brands with the most power are relevant, engaging, entertaining and more often than not courageous. They take a stand for or against something and more often than not have the confidence to stand apart from the crowd.

Your brand is one of the most important assets you possess to drive and differentiate your business. Every department in the company has a role to play in bringing the brand to life and ensure it is alive, vibrant and maximised.

## Brand UK: the impact of Brexit

The UK remains a top location to do business. However, perception of the UK as open for business is dropping. According to David Roth "Although Britain has a strong image globally in several areas including entrepreneurship, cultural influence and power it will need to be vigilant about its brand appeal on the world stage as Brexit further influences internal and external dynamics."

The good news is the UK's export market is booming. The latest figures show that for May 2017, total trade exports were £29.4bn, an increase of £2.9bn compared with the previous month and a rise of £5.9bn from May 2016. In total, exports were up 23% for Quarter one 2017 compared to Quarter one 2016 – a sum total of £86.9bn for the quarter (natwest).

Top tip: Watch Love brand Britain:

https://youtu.be/-rAKwdnmM4A

and Never has brand Britain being stronger in South East Asia:

https://youtu.be/lz77oXSLDCg

## Your Brand Power

As a brand owner, you have developed brand power as a result of growing your brand in your home market.   You have the right to decide where and when to sell your products. But, often, business owners forget this, and respond to ad hoc inquiries for their products, rather than thinking strategically and planning their export strategy.

So, just be aware, when you get flattering inquiries from overseas, whether it really fits with your wider strategy, and whether you really want to export to that country at this time.  Your strategy should inform everything your brand does, the actions you take, the places you appear and how you engage, educate and entertain your customers.

As a brand owner, when exporting, you can decide how to distribute your power, and many go for either an agent or distributor relationship.

So, let's discuss the distinction between agents and distributors. The main distinction is one of product ownership. With an agent, you will own the product, but the agent sells your product on your behalf, and you invoice the end customer.

With a distributor, a distributor will purchase directly from you, and then sell the products to their own customers. Distributorships are used as a low-risk means of expanding into overseas markets, whereas an agent is an intermediary with the authority to negotiate sales on your behalf.

Bonus: Watch my who holds the power video for more insights https://routesandbranches.com/who-holds-the-power/

*What are the advantages of using a distributor?*

Number one, the supplier can pass on the risk. Number two, the distributor is motivated to make the sale, as he's already purchased the goods from you. You have a reduced liability. You don't have to have a salesperson in the market, and you only need to monitor one account.

*What are the disadvantages of using a distributor?*

One, you have limited control. Local competition law governs your relationship. You have a lack of information about the end consumer. And, a distributor must be financially and commercially sound.

*What are the advantages of using an agent?*

When using an agent, the supplier has more control. Financial and commercial background is less crucial, and you have direct contact with your customers.

*What are the disadvantages of using an agent?*

Well, you cannot pass on risk. You have the liability for the actions of your agent. You must monitor all accounts with all end consumers. And, attention must be paid to legislation.

If you're looking for ways to increase your marketing power overseas, here's how to do it.

## Consumer Power

Know your customer. Consumers are powerful.

The speed at which fashions, trends, information and ideas travel around the globe is accelerating. As a result we are seeing the rise of the global consumer.

Consumers have two types of power. They can decide what to buy, and when to buy. This is their decision-making power, and it affects your international sales. Your first task is to understand your new international customers. Are they the same profile of customer as the UK? Do they have the same challenges or additional ones? Don't assume that the market is the same as home. How customers buy, who they buy from and who they trust to help – are all subtly yet importantly different from market to market (natwest.contentlive.co.uk).

Socially conscious consumers are seeking to use their voices and purchasing power to halt unsustainable business practices. Concerned consumers are realising that they can use social media to organise themselves around shared values to start effective movements. Social networking on computers and smartphones is common, regardless of the continent. Consumers are gravitating towards companies that are using social media to dialogue with them about social issues.

As you expand into new countries, you need to explore ways to connect with your new consumers using social media. One easy way to do this is to look for big events, calendar events or social events that are taking place which might encourage consumers to part with their cash at a certain time of year. For example, around the Formula One, or around Chinese New Year, or around big Hindu festivals, people are much more likely to make purchases. It's also great to talk to your consumers to get feedback about your product or service. This can help you to improve your product, and make it more appealing to more consumers.

Currency rates also affect consumer spending, with luxury brands beginning to rely on international shoppers.

## Government Power

Finally, let's talk about the power the government holds when exporting. Governments set regulation and legislation governing what you can export, how you can export, when you can export. And, it is important to be well briefed on these, and aware of all the documentation necessary in order to move your goods or services to a new market.

You may believe that your company is providing consumers with greater choice or a better product or service but the countries government may see your business as a threat to an industry or a source of tax revenue.

It's important that you are compliant with all the legislation in your own country, and also in the end destination, in order to export successfully.

In some countries, corruption within government can create challenges for exporters. In other's the government has a history of nationalising industries that they deem important to their national interest. The World Bank produces a ranking of ease of doing business. You may find it useful to refer to this when researching your markets.

# Step 5: Authority

Breaking into an international market is difficult. Many companies don't realize just how intricate breaking into an international market can be. Finding the right market—and staying objective—is imperative. Market research should be used to help understand the new market from multiple perspectives. Conducting a gap analysis can be a good indicator of where your company, brand and products may fit into the country you are trying to enter. Understanding the market and its economics is important, but having a grasp on the cultural norms, language and nuances within the culture is essential.

In this chapter, we are going to discuss how to become an expert or authority in your chosen market so that you can establish as presence not just as an exporter but as a thriving international brand.

## Why is it beneficial to become recognised as an expert or authority?

Those who are recognized as industry experts have a leg up in the business world. They command higher fees, open doors more easily and are often called upon by the media for quotes and feature stories (www.entrepreneur.com). Becoming an expert in your overseas market will make it easier for you to gain and maintain market share.

No matter what the size of your business, you've spent years developing the knowledge that makes your company a success. So why not maximise the return on your knowledge by leveraging it in a foreign market?

## So how do you become an authority?

A great way to become more valuable in your export market is to become an expert or the authority in your niche. The best way to prove you have something of value to share is to share it. First you need to evaluate your current position. What do you have that you could share? What do you know about the market right now? What market needs have you identified? Use your website and social media outlets to create a strong and authoritative online presence. Provide helpful information to your target audience, content that appeals to their wants, needs, and challenges (www.forbes.com).

A lot of business owners feel uncomfortable with the idea of calling themselves or their business an expert, but if you have an area of expertise that you can use to help others, it makes sense to tell people about it. Spend some time thinking about what your businesses specialist subject is. Try and pinpoint as niche an area as possible (The Guardian, 2015). One of the exercises Routes and Branches does with all of its customers is analyse the business strengths as this helps us to promote you to potential overseas partners.

You are probably already an expert, or close to one, at what you are currently doing, so you can easily build upon that expertise and take it to the next level. Some of the ways you could do that are:

1. Become a member of the leading associations and organizations related to your industry. Go deeper by joining the board of directors, volunteering, speaking or sponsoring various events.

2. Look for opportunities to author articles about your industry. Provide articles or news items for organization or association newsletters or publications, pitch focused article ideas to your industry's trade magazines, and scan the news for topics to which you can add information as an industry expert. Use these as opportunities to really show off your knowledge. Don't be scared of giving away some content for free – it'll be worth it

3. If your industry appears in national news, pitch topic ideas to the editors of online and print publications, or to the news director at broadcast media. Tell them why your topic is important now, why it will impact their readers or viewers and why you are the person who should tell the story (www.entrepreneur.com).

4. Don't simply write a few articles here and there, but instead commit to regular content creation for a variety of outlets, as it helps build up your personal brand faster (Brian Horn, 2018).

5. Give speeches or participate in seminars and panels. Hone your speaking skills, study voice projection and observe other engaging speakers.

The more valuable content you publish, the more you'll establish your brand as an authority in your field. Part of having authority status is being both an educator and an advocate for your clients. The key is to consistently add value.

Use social media to:

- Answer questions
- Join industry conversations
- Share relevant content

Remember it's about helping your audience not you. They have problems, and you have advice that can help them.

Becoming an expert takes work. You are going to have to put a lot of work and dedication into it. In his book Outliers, Malcolm Gladwell says that it takes about ten thousand hours of practice to achieve mastery in a particular field.

Bonus: For more tips on how to establish your brand authority and market your business successfully overseas watch my authority video on my blog:

https://routesandbranches.com/business-export-success-05-business-authority-successful-marketing/

## Before you export put strong foundations in place by developing expertise in your home market

When you think about how to grow your business, the first thing that probably comes to mind is getting new customers (www.thebalance.com/). But the customers you already have are your best bet for increasing your sales; it's easier and more cost-effective to get people who are already buying from you to buy more than to find new customers and persuade them to buy from you

David Epstein put it simply: "The hallmark of expertise is figuring out what information is important." When expanding into a new market the most important thing to do is to establish what are the needs of your consumers? What adaptations will you need to make to your product to meet their needs? What information do they want to see on your packaging? What messages do they want to read or hear in your marketing that would make them buy your product?

What can you do to further develop your expertise:

- Market research,
- Reading books,
- Online courses,
- Watching videos,
- Attending seminars and training programs,
- Learning from other experts within the field,
- Start exporting,
- Share your knowledge.

*Scale your national business*

The best businesses are started as a means to fill a need. Their inspiration tends to come from facing a problem and realizing that a solution doesn't exist yet, or creating a demand for a service people need but didn't even know they wanted. But how do you get from this point to growing a business that will thrive internationally? Scaling your business is hard. It takes considerable effort.

In the beginning you will wear many hats. From sales to marketing to finance to compliance, you'll likely be involved in all aspects of the business.

The first way to grow your business is to build and develop your sales funnel. Before you create a sales funnel you need to carefully conceptualise each step of the process. Have your call to action in mind. What do you want your customer to do? How are you adding value to them?

Top tip: make a record of your answers to these questions and revisit it regularly.

### Keep organised

'Fail to plan, plan to fail' is the maxim doing the rounds in business circles. Because it's true. People have their own ways of planning – for some, it means scribbling things down on a piece of paper once in a while; for others, methodical and detailed plans are what gets them through. Choose a planning method that works for you, but plan all the same. Keep records and contracts organised so that you have them to hand when you need them. Always know where you are in your business – financially and strategically – because it will make a huge difference. Also, don't take on too much and burn out – learn when to say 'no', so that you have the space to provide a good service and do your job well.

Utilize technology to facilitate your growth. A customer management system can help you to scale quickly without cumbersome manual tracking.

### Identify new opportunities

Analyse new opportunities in your business by understanding your demographic better. Think of new ways to present your products or services, so that your clients are happy, and will come back for more or tell others. Even in today's tech-heavy world, word-of-mouth is a powerful force.

### Put Training and development at the heart of your growth strategy

All businesses have access to an extensive pool of knowledge - whether this is their understanding of customers' needs and the business environment or the skills and experience of staff.

The way a business gathers, shares and exploits this knowledge can be central to its ability to develop successfully. Knowledge management can benefit all businesses.

You've probably done market research into the need for your business to exist in the first place. If nobody wanted what you're selling, you wouldn't be trading. You can tailor this market knowledge to target particular customers with specific types of product or service.

Having staff who are knowledgeable can be invaluable in setting you apart from competitors. You should make sure that your employees' knowledge and skills are passed on to their colleagues and successors wherever possible

Your sources of business knowledge include:

- Customer knowledge
- Employee and supplier relationships
- Market knowledge
- Knowledge of the business environment
- Professional associations
- Trade exhibitions and conferences
- Product research and development
- Organisational memory
- Non-executive directors

You can scale your business by exploiting your knowledge.

- Use your knowledge to improve your goods and services
- Increase customer satisfaction
- Increase the quality of your suppliers
- Improve productivity
- Improve recruitment and retention
- Sell or licence your knowledge to others

One of the best ways to scale your business is to make knowledge central to your business vision. Which in practice means developing a business culture based on knowledge sharing. Knowledge sharing is essential to avoid skills being lost when individuals leave or retire. One of the ways to create a knowledge sharing culture might be to offer incentives to staff who generate useful market news or suggest ways to better serve your customers. I speak more about making knowledge central to your vision on my blog.

You should also make sure that you adequately protect your company's intellectual property (IP)

### Build a solid network

It's important to build a network of other professionals and businesses to help you grow. Business owners often think of networking as connecting with potential clients, but connecting with other services providers can bring referrals as well as opportunities to collaborate in the future.

You can read more about how to create a solid network on our blog www.routesandbranches.com/blog

### Using Brand Britain

The statement "made in Britain" carries a lot of kudos with some overseas customers. Demand for goods that are 'Made in Britain' and a willingness for key markets to pay a premium for these goods should be factored into the return on investment equation undertaken by UK firms. (https://www.barclayscorporate.com)

In emerging high growth markets such as China customers perceive British goods to be better quality and value for money. This translates to a willingness to pay a premium for British made goods. Anecdotally, UK businesses are revered for their integrity, and there is a general perception that British made products are to be trusted. Britain also has a reputation for innovation and quality. Many emerging markets are members of the commonwealth where English is widely spoken and British made goods are more familiar.

So how can you cash in on that positive association?

Consider creating micro-sites targeted at particular countries, then link back to translated versions of your main site. Encourage site visitors to post their comments and recommendations.

### Consumer Confidence

Price is considered one of the most important factors affecting the consumers' perception of a product. Once consumers perceive a price difference between local and foreign items, price differentials begin to affect their preference for local goods.

A high-priced item may be perceived of being high in quality because of the image created by manufacturers through advertising. Similarly, a global product may be perceived to be of superior quality as quality is believed to be a prerequisite for international acceptance.

It is believed that people, especially the young ones, consider current fashions and trends while buying a product.

The attitudes and perceptions of consumers toward their choice of goods sometimes depends on categories, for example, electronic goods from Italy may be perceived as a poor quality but Italian clothing would be perceived as fashionable and high quality. And the Japanese electronic goods would be perceived with positive attitudes while their clothing will be negatively perceived.

Patriotic consumers believe that our local companies have a competitive edge over their foreign competitors because they are closer to consumers here and have a better understanding of what people want.

*Effective Marketing*

International marketing isn't just about translating your brochures into another language. It's about having a plan based upon a realistic assessment of what your company wants to achieve. An analysis of which markets make the most sense then a framework or blueprint of how you will get the work done.

Selling overseas requires you to navigate unfamiliar cultures and values. But don't let that discourage you. By learning how to effectively advertise in the international arena, your business can access untapped markets, reach new customers and reap high rewards.

The first step is to identify an appropriate overseas market. Your approach will need to be focused and purposeful. Locate regions or cities where your product can fill a gap or satisfy an unmet need. Your research must include thorough analysis of your target countries legal and regulatory structures. Many nations have strict laws about what can be included in an advertisement. National laws around marketing often differ between industries.

When designing content look what works for you domestically and then adapt it to meet the new market. Your content marketing should help prospects understand if you're the right fit by showing what it's like to work with you. It should also increase your prospects familiarity with your brand by appearing regularly in front of them. It should also be used to help you to develop their trust by demonstrating your expertise.

Here are some top tips to help you maximise your content strategy:

- Choose methods where you have an execution advantage
- You also need to market effectively to the person or people who make the decision to hire you
- First and foremost, seek out an audience that is representative of your target market
- Choose Your Topics Wisely
- Start by determining what potential clients actually want to know about.
- Your content should be localized, and written in a voice that accounts for regional preferences and differences.

If you want to reach a global audience, one of the most important things you can do is optimize your website for international users. Do your colours and graphics have an acceptable, positive connotation in your target market? If you sell directly from your website, do you offer a currency-conversion plugin to display the relevant cost in an alternate currency? Is your site optimized to display properly on mobile, and does it still display properly even after it's machine-translated by a service like Google or Bing? Carefully consider the needs of your target market and let these facts dictate your site optimization, not the other way around.

# Step 6: Legitimacy

A business is legitimate if it is compliant. In international trade, "compliance" refers to how well a company observes the laws and regulations that govern its international business operations. Many of these rules are established by national governments to manage their countries' trade with other nations while others are created to fulfil the requirements of international trade agreements

If you get compliance right, there is every reason for the export to be delivered on time and without extra costs, fines or penalties.

If you're an exporter or importer, you need a clear understanding of the rules that govern international trade in your sector. This is important to avoid risk. The right paperwork is crucial. Missing or inaccurate documents can increase risks, lead to delays and extra costs, or even prevent a deal from being completed.

Failing to comply with trade rules, even accidentally, can lead to serious consequences. Non-compliance, can lead to missed deadlines, unexpected costs that eat into profits, the need for management time to be spent on sorting problems, late delivery, and in some cases, prison. It's the customer who loses out in the short term. Longer term, the exporter loses his reputation for being a reliable business partner. (BExA)

You are responsible for ensuring that all export documentation is properly completed and is submitted to customs authorities in a timely manner.

- There should be a clear written contract between buyer and seller, including details of exactly where goods will be delivered
- Specific documents may be needed to get the goods through customs and to work out the right duty and tax charges. There may be requirements both for the country the goods are being exported from and the country they are being imported into

- Documentation is needed to cover the transport of the goods and insurance during the journey
- The right paperwork can be an important part of the payment mechanism

You need to ensure that your export operations process is as streamlined and efficient as possible. It is important to understand the needs of your overseas customers. To avoid costly penalties or border delays make sure that your compliance team is on top of the latest export requirements for each country that you ship to. Most compliance is a combination of common sense, good teamwork and record keeping. Set your standards high, play by the rules and be sufficiently nimble so you can accommodate, or even take advantage of rule changes.

Many businesses use the services of freight forwarder or import agent. The British International Freight Association (BIFA) may be able to identify a suitable freight forwarder.

## Incoterms

Fifty nine countries worldwide are signatories to the U.N. Convention on Contract for the International Sale of Goods ("CISG") (The Guardian). The purpose of the CISG is to bring uniformity to international business transactions principally with respect to commonly used trade terms.

Incoterms were developed in 1939 by the International Chamber of Commerce ("ICC"), and are pre-defined commercial terms which have been accepted by traders and governments worldwide to explain important terms such as insurance, carriage or risk of loss widely used in international commercial transactions.

Incoterms were developed in 1939 by the International Chamber of Commerce ("ICC"), and are pre-defined commercial terms which have been accepted by traders and governments worldwide to explain important terms such as insurance, carriage or risk of loss widely used in international commercial transactions.

The contract should set out where the goods are being delivered. It should cover who is responsible for every stage of the journey, including customs clearance, and what insurance is required. It should also make it clear who pays for each different cost.

To avoid confusion, internationally agreed Incoterms should be used to spell out exactly what delivery terms are being agreed, such as:

- where the goods will be delivered
- who arranges transport
- who is responsible for insuring the goods, and who pays for insurance
- who handles customs procedures, and who pays any duties and taxes

Incoterms will not apply to the terms of the insurance contract. They will not apply to the terms of financing or to the terms negotiated for carriage or transportation of the equipment. Incoterms are primarily used for equipment sold for delivery across international boundaries. They will not address the consequences of a breach of contract or exemptions of liability. Incoterms relate to the terms between the exporter and importer.

Here are the main responsibilities and obligations:

- Point of delivery: here, the incoterms defines the point of change of hands from seller to buyer.
- Transportation costs: here, the incoterms defines who pays for whichever transportation is required.
- Export and import formalities: here, incoterms defines which party arranges for import and export formalities.
- Insurance cost: here, incoterms define who takes charge of the insurance cost.

Advantages of using incoterms:

As they stand today, there are eleven main terms and a number of secondary terms that help buyers and sellers communicate the provisions of a contract in a clearer way; therefore, reducing the risk of misinterpretation by one of the parties.

Incoterms govern everything from transportation costs, insurance to liabilities. They contribute to answering questions such as "When will the delivery be completed?" "What are the modalities and conditions for transportation?" and "How do you ensure one party that the other has met the established standards?

### Trade in services

With no physical delivery of the product, contracts in services cannot use Incoterms. Instead, the key issue tends to be defining exactly what services are being provided and to what standards. Rules on the international supply of services changed on 28 December 2009. You may be required to supply extra information to customers including how your services work, how you handle complaints, and how you apply principles of non-discrimination.

### Records

You're required to keep records for all traded goods you declare to HMRC for four years, for duty and tax purposes and for government statistics.

If you keep archived trade documents on your premises you should make every effort to secure them. Your premises should always be locked when not in use and you could consider additional locking of cabinets and storage rooms.

### Exporting goods outside of the EU

If you export goods to countries outside the EU (known as 'third countries'), you must have the appropriate licences and make export declarations to customs through the National Export System (NES). You must also make sure that VAT, import taxes and duties in the destination country are paid where necessary, and follow transport procedures, though this is normally the responsibility of the importing person or company.

## Exporting goods in the EU

If you are selling goods within the EU, most goods are in free circulation and can be freely moved from the UK to other EU countries without customs controls or charges. It's good practice to accompany shipments with a commercial invoice and a packing list

## International transport documentation

Transport documentation is needed to provide instructions to the carrier on what should be done with the goods. They can be used to pass responsibility for, and sometimes ownership of, the goods during their journey.

If you are exporting goods, you typically complete an Export Cargo Shipping Instruction giving the freight forwarder details of the goods and how they are to reach their destination.

You also normally complete a Standard Shipping Note, telling the port how to handle the goods.

The carrier should provide you with documentary evidence that they have received the goods, e.g. a bill of lading or a waybill. You should keep any documents as evidence in case of later problems with the shipment.

A CIM Consignment Note gives details of the goods being transported. If you are shipping dangerous goods, you must also complete a dangerous goods declaration.

## International trade documentation and payments

Documentary collections and documentary credits are payment methods often used in international trade. By using special paperwork, the risks of the customer failing to pay or the supplier failing to deliver are reduced:

With a documentary collection, the exporter prepares a bill of exchange stating how much is to be paid and when. Once the customer accepts this bill of exchange, they are legally liable for payment. Only then does the exporter, usually through the bank in the overseas country, allow the customer to have the transport documents needed to take possession of the goods.

With a documentary credit, the customer arranges a letter of credit from their bank. The bank agrees to pay the exporter once all the right documentation - such as transport documents showing the right goods have been despatched - is received. The exporter must provide the required paperwork within the agreed time limit and with no discrepancies.

# Step 7: A thriving business

Throughout the book I have explored the challenges facing exporters and how to overcome those challenges. The book walked you through the first 6 steps in my seven step process to successful export. In this chapter we pull all of that knowledge together to map out a roadmap for export success and create a blueprint for a thriving international business.

In the introduction I argue that there was a necessary paradigm shift in our thinking to enable thriving international businesses, a thriving global economy, and a thriving world. I set out three questions:

1. What are our values as a nation?

2. What place do business owners want to hold in the world?

3. As a nation is the UK brave enough to be the change we wish to see in the world? Are we ready to define our values, assert them and chart our course? Is this a pivotal moment in history? I believe so.

I want to live in a global society that values people, and takes care of our planet. A society where we exchange knowledge with one another; one where we laugh together, play together, share with one another. I want to work with business owners who share this aspiration and who see their businesses as facilitators of these goals. Business owners that are passionate about thriving globally. This is the big change I aspire to and the reason for calling the book Export, Thrive, Change the World. Though I think how to change the world might need to be book two!

*A blueprint for thriving globally*

Expanding your service or product overseas can take your business to another level. If you're successful, it can transform it. Exporting offers the prospect of new markets, more sales, better profits and a greater spread of customers. But if you are not ready it can be extremely damaging and in some cases fatal.

The first step is to make sure you are "Export ready". I have created an export readiness checklist which is available to download from my website. (www.routesandbranches.com)

## Let's recap: What would it look like to have a thriving planet?

Humanity's twenty-first century challenge is to meet the needs of all within the means of the planet. In other words, to ensure that no one falls short on life's essentials (from food and housing to healthcare and political voice), while ensuring that collectively global society does not overshoot our pressure on Earth's life-supporting systems, on which we fundamentally depend – such as a stable climate, fertile soils, and a protective ozone layer. To run a thriving business in the twenty-first century is to operate within these parameters.

Although Earth has undergone many periods of significant environmental change, the planet's environment has been unusually stable for the past ten thousand years (www.nature.com). This period of stability — known to geologists as the Holocene — has seen human civilizations arise, develop and thrive. Such stability may now be under threat. Since the Industrial Revolution, a new era has arisen, the Anthropocene (www.nature.com), in which human actions have become the main driver of global environmental change. This could see human activities push the Earth system outside the stable environmental state of the Holocene, with consequences that are detrimental or even catastrophic for large parts of the world (www.nature.com).

I believe as business owners we have a responsibility not to exacerbate this problem. I also believe we are capable of creating the conditions for a thriving planet and we can do this by creating thriving international businesses. I believe we can change the world in a positive way by changing our business practices. That starts with changing our business metrics and values.

## The three pillars: Purpose, People and Profit

Traditionally business advisors and consultants use a three-pillar system to explain the process of creating a growing business. I have taken a slightly different approach; my aim is to help you create a sustainable thriving international business. But broadly speaking my seven steps can be fitted into the three-pillar approach, I have chosen to move people to the bottom and span it across all categories as I don't think a thriving business can thrive unless people are at the heart of everything you do.

So here is my model for success:

| Purpose | | | Profit | | | |
|---------|--------|------|--------|-----------|------------|----------------------------------|
| Values  | Vision | Fear | Power  | Authority | Legitimacy | A thriving international business |
| People | | | | | | |

Throughout this book I argue that export success comes as a result of comprehensively following steps; don't try to take shortcuts. Here is a summary of the main steps:

- Assess whether or not you are export ready using the Routes and Branches assessment tool.
- Understand your values and question whether they are serving you.
- Thorough market research – I cannot stress the importance of this one enough! Bonus: Read our blog to find out why market research is so important https://routesandbranches.com/why-market-research-matters-to-businesses/
- Determine your Route to market.
- Identify and due diligence check potential partners.
- Create a financial plan.
- Create a strategic plan including logistics.
- Create a marketing plan.
- Make sure each of your plans are compatible with one another.

- Make sure each of your plans are compatible with your domestic business.
- Implement your plans.
- Review, revise, redo – ask for help when you need it.

Bonus: Visit our blog to learn how to manage your business logistics effectively https://routesandbranches.com/top-7-tips-help-manage-small-business-logistics-effectively/

## A word of warning

If your business is failing domestically it is unlikely to succeed overseas. Before trying to compete overseas you should take corrective action to improve your domestic business. You need to examine and admit the failings in your domestic business and work to rectify these before you move on to overseas markets or you will create a systemic problem for yourself.

## Assess whether or not you are export ready

To run a successful business your purpose of existing must be meaningful and tangible. It is critical to analyse your motives for entering overseas markets. (Earlier in the book and in our Routes course I share how to do this.) A purpose is the big picture and your reason for existing. We discussed in depth purpose, values and vision in the early chapters of the book. To export successfully you must be able to see your business as you want it to be in five or ten years time. You must understand what you are trying to achieve and why. You must be able to communicate this why to others. Your brand values need to be entrenched into the whole business and understood by everyone that works for you. They must also be understood and appreciated by your customers.

In order to achieve sustainable success, companies must repeatedly re-examine their sense of purpose and values and make sure the organisation serves it well. Before we can look at our values and prioritizations and change them into better, healthier ones, we must first become uncertain of our current values (Manson, The Subtle Art of Not Giving a F*ck:). It's a continuous process of improvement.

Your sense of purpose will determine the way you're your structure your business. Business models and structures are different to facilitate different business outcomes. An exporting business will require a different business model to one who is not exporting.

- What are the implications of your vision on your business model?
- How will your vision influence the way you structure your business?

### Thorough Market Research

Throughout the book I have stressed the importance of thorough market research, it is fundamental to your export success. Spending time on research will prevent you from making costly mistakes elsewhere.

Make sure to include a risk analysis in your research and use your findings to guide management decisions including how to manage the identified risks. No export market is risk free so it's important to do this.

If you are gasping at the thought of market research, Routes and Branches can help you. You will find information on our services page.

### Determine your Route to market

Earlier in the book I discuss in detail how to find the right route to market for your product and service. In summary, in order to determine the most appropriate route to market for your business you need to consider how and where your customers shop. You also need to consider how much it will cost and whether you have the resources and ability to manage this channel. By analysing the different route to market options against these criteria you will be able to determine which is most appropriate for your business. There may not be a perfect solution as all international expansion comes with some risk.

Identify appropriate partners

Identifying appropriate partners in the market is one of the most critical stages for successful exporters. It is vitally important that you establish a good relationship with your partner overseas, as they will be fundamental in delivering your brand promises to your customers. But identifying the right partner can be challenging particularly if you are new to exporting and have little or no export experience. That's where working with an advisor such as Routes and Branches or an international trade advisor provided by The Department of International Trade or ideally both can save you time, money and stress.

There are also some excellent resources online to help you to get started. These include:

1. GlobalTrade.net Globaltrade.net is one of the preeminent international trade directories on the web, with roughly one hundred and forty nine thousand import and export service providers worldwide listed on its site (Tradeready.ca).

2. Globality.com is a trade directory that is geared towards connecting larger multinational corporations with small to midsized businesses.

3. Europages is a premier trade directories for European businesses, with a list of over 2.6 million businesses, primarily located in Europe.

The question all new exporters seek to answer is: What constitutes a suitable partner, and how do I find a good overseas partner with limited staff, time and resources?

- Qualities to look out for:
- A representative or partner with a large existing customer base.
- Someone who is looking to add a company like yours to their line.
- Make sure you are comfortable with communicating with them and also the way that they communicate as they will represent you at an international level.

- Check their portfolio and follow up to get references.
- You need to be comfortable that they are capable of doing what they say they will be doing.
- Make sure they are comfortable selling your product. alongside the other companies they represent.
- Get legal/professional assistance to prepare a partner agreement.
- Ask the representative for an assessment of the in-country market potential of your products.
- I recommend that you do not grant exclusivity until the representative has demonstrated their capability.
- Do not hesitate to ask potential partners detailed and specific questions.

Once you have identified a long list of potential partners you need to narrow it down. Weed out any that have not worked with a UK, US, or EU business before as they may not be ready to meet the quality standards that you expect. Look for a partner with previous experience and try to confirm with their previous clients if they were happy or not. It is vital that you also conduct thorough due diligence and I highly recommend using professional service providers to do this. Once you have conducted your due diligence on the recommended three shortlisted firms consider hiring two simultaneously so that you can compare and measure the consistency of their service.

Be prepared to relinquish tactical decisions to foreign partners so they can move quickly on the ground. They know the local culture better than you do.

To avoid a bad partnership you should consider the following things (Entrepreneur.com):

- Trust.
- Friendship.
- Probation period/trial run.
- Partner employee or consultant.
- Complementary strengths.
- Balanced responsibilities.

- Money.

## Create a Financial Plan

Financial analysis is an important part of export planning. If the financial analysis is not done, how will you know when and if you will be profitable.

When performing a financial analysis it is important to be realistic with your numbers. You do not want to use the "best case scenario" for all your projections. Instead you should weigh all the variables and use moderate numbers.

- What are your financial targets?
- What are your financial targets for your exporting efforts—costs, product pricing and cash flow?
- Have you taken into account the possibility of longer payment cycles, higher cost of sales and the cost of risk protection?

Financial planning is covered in our Routes course which is available to purchase on our website: www.routesandbranches.com

## Create a Strategic Plan

I believe that for a business to thrive, it must have a solid plan to ensure it is commercially viable from the beginning. You must plan to be profitable and you must adopt a commercially viable business model.

An export strategy is a component of your business plan that identifies your global business aims and objectives and develops an action plan to achieve them. Make sure everyone in the company involved in achieving export results is aware of the plan and has a sense of engagement with it.

Developing a sound export strategy helps you define your export aims and match your resources to those aims. Your export strategy will help you manage the market sectors you have identified as core business. Focusing your resources enables you to provide quality responses and service to your new export customers.

Bonus: Visit my blog https://routesandbranches.com/the-ultimate-guide-on-how-to-write-your-export-strategy/ for more information about how to create your export strategy

As you know each market has its own nuances due to economic, cultural, governmental, and market conditions. It is important to develop a localized strategy and business plan that drives local success while remaining integrated with the overall corporate strategy and objectives for each of your overseas markets.

Your export plan is a working document that should be modified as you gain access to new information.

Having now read the majority of the book; what is your business vision? Do you feel inspired and empowered to export? What is holding you back?

## In light of Brexit what should I be doing now to ensure my business thrives?

Throughout the book I talk about three main steps to ensure that you can create a thriving international business. Step one is to ensure that you invest in your home market and make that business successful first. Focus on establishing a brand reputation for the right reasons. Next is market research, this is critical to success. Before embarking on any overseas ventures make sure that there is a demand for your product or service and that you fully understand the new environment in which you intend to operate. Finally be honest and realistic about the barriers to entry and doing business. Analyse your risks and make sure you have plans in place to mitigate against them. Ask for help where you need it.

With Brexit fast approaching all British Business owners need to be doing the following things to ensure that they can continue to operate successfully post Brexit. (Dechert):

- Reviewing and identifying aspects of the business that rely on, or assume the applicability of, pan-EU arrangements such as EU rules of origin and customs procedures, passporting for financial services, EU-wide medicine licenses, etc.

- Understanding the actual (or likely) position of the UK, the EU Governments and EU institutions on the contents of the exit agreement, as well as the ambitions for the future UK-EU trading relationship.
- Establishing what the UK's baseline obligations in the WTO and other international bodies means for your business.
- Identifying EU laws which currently impact both your operations and that of your wider industry.
- Identifying the nature and extent of interaction with pan-EU agencies.
- Considering a government relations strategy (whether directly or through an industry group). Identify key proposals or considerations. Make these reasoned, evidence-based, granular and ambitious, while taking account of political realities. Respond to government consultations.
- Considering the impact on your supply chains and customer base.
- Looking at the nuts and bolts of your business including your data protection obligations; contractual terms; employment rights; intellectual property plans; and on-going litigation.

# Conclusions

I said at the beginning of the book that in the wake of Brexit we need to go back to our values as a nation and re-establish our place in the world. In doing so business owners need to step up and lead the way "to be the change we wish to see in the world". It's time to be brave. To step out of our comfort zones and begin to address the challenges that lie before us with creative balanced solutions that benefit not just us as an individual, company, or even country but us as a global society of interconnected human beings.

My vision is for us (Business owners and entrepreneurs) to create a thriving global economy and society. I believe export is a mechanism and a process to help us to extend our reach and grow our audience, so that as businesses we can maximise the impact of our solutions. I believe that as business owners we need to give our visions and values an audience. That we need to make it our priority to attract attention to a way of operating that supports our planet and the people on it to thrive.

That is my big vision.

I wrote this book from the perspective that you like me regardless of how you voted, view Brexit as an opportunity for change and are ready to embrace the change and the potential to thrive that comes with it.

I hope you share my vision, and I hope that Routes and Branches can support you to realise your exporting ambitions, no matter what challenges you face.

# Contact Us

For more information about how Jennifer can support your business to succeed please email Jennifer@routesandbranches.com or visit our website www.routesandbranches.com. You will also find us on social media, LinkedIn, Facebook, Twitter and Youtube as well as our podcast Routes and Branches: The Exporters podcast.

# Glossary

**CFR** – cost and freight

**CFS** – container freight station

**CIF** – Cost insurance and freight

**CIP** – Carriage and insurance paid

**CPT** – Carriage paid to

**DAT** – Delivered at terminal

**DAP** – Delivered at place

**DDP**- Delivered duty paid

**DDU** – Delivered Duty Unpaid

**Demurrage** refers to the charges that the charterer pays to the ship owner for its delayed operations of loading/unloading.

**DEQ** – Delivered Ex Quay

**Direct selling:** Direct selling is where you sell your product straight to the customer, without a middle man - through your own website, door-to-door, using direct marketing or advertising, or through your own shop.

**Distance sales:** This is where you sell to customers remotely - usually through a website, telesales or direct mail such as catalogues and brochures. It's much cheaper than renting retail space and you don't have to travel to customers, saving time and money.

**Ecological ceiling issues:**

Climate change

- Ocean acidification
- Chemical pollution
- Nitrogen and phosphorus loading
- Freshwater withdrawals
- Land conversion

- Biodiversity loss
- Air pollution
- Ozone layer depletion

**Export Licenses:** An export license is a government document that authorizes the export of specific goods in specific quantities to a particular destination.

**EXW** – ex works

**FAS** – free alongside ship

**FCA** – free carrier

**FCL** – full container load

**FOB** – free on board

**LCL** – less than container load

**Online sales:** There are different ways to sell your product online - such as through your own website, by using affiliate marketing, through an auction site such as Ebay, through a retailer's website, through online adverts, or using direct emailing to a customer database

**PO** – Purchase Order

**Selling wholesale:** You sell your product to a retailer, wholesaler or reseller, who then sells it on to consumers.

**SME:** Small and Medium sized Enterprise

The usual definition of small and medium sized enterprises (SMEs) is any business with fewer than 250 employees. There were 5.7 million SMEs in the UK in 2017, which was over 99% of all businesses.

Service Export: Trade in services records the value of services exchanged between residents and non-residents of an economy, including services provided through foreign affiliates established abroad.

**Social foundation:**

- Water
- Food
- Health
- Education
- Income and work
- Peace and justice
- Political voice
- Social equity
- Gender equality
- Housing
- Networks
- Energy

**Tramp Shipping:** A boat or ship engaged in the tramp trade is one, which does not have a fixed schedule or published ports of call. As opposed to freight liners, tramp ships trade on the spot market with no fixed schedule or itinerary/ports-of-call(s).

# Bibliography

BExA. (n.d.). *Export Compliance*. Retrieved 07 19, 2018 from http://www.bexa.co.uk: http://www.bexa.co.uk/docs/BExA%20Guide%20to%20Export%20Compliance.pdf

Brian Horn, H. P. (2018). *7 steps to becoming a recognised expert in your industry.* Retrieved 07 16, 2018 from /www.huffingtonpost.com: https://www.huffingtonpost.com/brian-horn/7-steps-to-becoming-a-rec_b_8963042.html

Chamber International. (2018, 07 09). *7 point export strategy.* Retrieved 07 09, 2018 from www.chamber-international.com: https://www.chamber-international.com/exporting-chamber-international/new-exporters/our-7-point-export-strategy/

Dechert. (n.d.). *www.dechert.com*. Retrieved 07 10, 2018 from Brexit resource centre: https://www.dechert.com/knowledge/hot-topic/brexit-resource-center.html?gclid=EAIaIQobChMI-azyp5uU3AIVxlRwCh2WxgeREAAYASAAEgLwmPD_BwE

Deloitte. (2014). *Business trends.* Retrieved 07 22, 2018 from www2.deloitte.com: https://www2.deloitte.com/insights/us/en/focus/business-trends/2014/business-social-impact.html

Deloitte. (2014). *Business Trends.* Retrieved 07 22, 2018 from https://www2.deloitte.com: https://www2.deloitte.com/insights/us/en/focus/business-trends/2014/business-social-impact.html#endnote-11

Deloitte. (2014). *Business Trends.* Retrieved 07 22, 2018 from https://www2.deloitte.com: https://www2.deloitte.com/insights/us/en/focus/business-trends/2014/business-social-impact.html#endnote-11

Entrepreneur.com. (n.d.). Retrieved 08 14, 2018 from https://www.entrepreneur.com/article/273813

Federation of Small Business. (2016). *Destination export report 2016.* Retrieved 07 02, 2018 from www.fsb.org.uk: https://www.fsb.org.uk/docs/default-source/Publications/reports/fsb-destination-export-report-2016.pdf?sfvrsn=0

Federation of Small Business. (2016). *FSB Destination Export 2016.* Retrieved 07 02, 2018 from www.fsb.org.uk: https://www.fsb.org.uk/docs/default-source/Publications/reports/fsb-destination-export-report-2016.pdf?sfvrsn=0

Federation of Small Business. (2016). *FSB Destination Export Report 2016.* Retrieved 07 02, 2018 from www.fsb.org.uk: https://www.fsb.org.uk/docs/default-source/Publications/reports/fsb-destination-export-report-2016.pdf?sfvrsn=0

Federation of Small Business. (2016). *FSB Destination Export Report 2016.* Retrieved 07 02, 2018 from www.fsb.org.uk: https://www.fsb.org.uk/docs/default-source/Publications/reports/fsb-destination-export-report-2016.pdf?sfvrsn=0

Federation of small business. (2016). *www.fsb.org.uk.* Retrieved 07 02, 2018 from FSB destination export report 2016: https://www.fsb.org.uk/docs/default-source/Publications/reports/fsb-destination-export-report-2016.pdf?sfvrsn=0

https://www.barclayscorporate.com. (n.d.). *insight-and-research/trading-and-exporting/brand-britain.html.* Retrieved 08 16, 2018 from https://www.barclayscorporate.com:

https://www.barclayscorporate.com/insight-and-research/trading-and-exporting/brand-britain.html

Jack Canfield. (n.d.). *How to create an empowering vision book.* Retrieved 07 02, 2018 from jackcanfield.com: http://jackcanfield.com/blog/how-to-create-an-empowering-vision-book/

Jack Canfield. (n.d.). *How to create an empowering vision book.* Retrieved 07 02, 2018 from www.jackcanfield.com: http://jackcanfield.com/blog/how-to-create-an-empowering-vision-book/

Joel Comm. (n.d.). *everything you need to know about social enterprise.* Retrieved 07 22, 2018 from www.inc.com: https://www.inc.com/joel-comm/everything-you-need-to-know-about-social-enterprises.html

Kate Raworth. (n.d.). *A safe and just space for humanity.* Retrieved 07 22, 2018 from oxfam discussion papers: oxfam.org

Kate Raworth. (2017, 04 16). *Spring Renewal Bring on Regenerative Economics.* Retrieved 07 02, 2018 from www.kateraworth.com: https://www.kateraworth.com/2017/04/16/spring-renewal-bring-on-regenerative-economics/

Kate Raworth. (2018, 07 04). TED Talks Daily in Podcasts. *https://itunes.apple.com/in/podcast/healthy-economy-should-be-designed-to-thrive-not-grow/id160904630?i=1000411486259&mt=2*
.

Mahatma Gandhi. (n.d.). Retrieved 07 22, 2018

Manson, M. *The Subtle Art of Not Giving a F\*ck: A Counterintuitive Approach to Living a Good Life .* HarperCollins. Kindle Edition.

Manson, M. *The Subtle Art of Not Giving a F*ck: A Counterintuitive Approach to Living a Good Life* . (H. K. Edition., Ed.) HarperCollins. Kindle Edition.

Manson, M. *The Subtle Art of Not Giving a F*ck: A Counterintuitive Approach to Living a Good Life* . HarperCollins. Kindle Edition. .

Manson, M. *The Subtle Art of Not Giving a F*ck: A Counterintuitive Approach to Living a Good Life* . HarperCollins. Kindle Edition.

Marketing Consultancy Division. (n.d.). *Export bullitin no 1*. Retrieved 07 02, 2018 from www.sidf.gov.sa: https://www.sidf.gov.sa/en/MediaCenter/ResearchandStudies/Exp ortInformationExportBulletinKnowledgeBase/2003-EB-01-Export%20Strategy.pdf

Mcmahon, L. (n.d.). *Small business administration exports only*. Retrieved 07 02, 2018 from www.inc.com: https://www.inc.com/associated-press/linda-mcmahon-small-business-administration-exports-only-1-percent-small-business.html

natwest. (n.d.). *natwest.contentlive.co.uk*. Retrieved 07 23, 2018 from http://natwest.contentlive.co.uk/content/5209a186-5624-ab13-aab4-9a1800db7443.

natwest.contentlive.co.uk. (n.d.). *content*. Retrieved 07 22, 2018 from natwest.contentlive.co.uk: http://natwest.contentlive.co.uk/content/5209a186-5624-ab13-aab4-9a1800db7443

Social Media Week. (2016, 06). *Attention new currency get content fully absorbed*. Retrieved 07 02, 2018 from socialmediaweek.org: https://socialmediaweek.org/blog/2016/06/attention-new-currency-get-content-fully-absorbed-consumers/

Startups UK. (n.d.). *63 of small business export*. Retrieved 07 02, 2018 from www.startups.co.uk: https://startups.co.uk/63-of-small-businesses-export/

Surrey University. (n.d.). *Success in Challenging times full findings*. Retrieved 07 02, 2018 from www.surrey.ac.uk: https://www.surrey.ac.uk/sbs/files/Success_in_Challenging_Times_Full_Findings.pdf

Taylor Wessing. (2018). *Global Intellectual Property Index 5th Report*. Retrieved 07 16, 2018 from Taylor Wessing: https://united-kingdom.taylorwessing.com/documents/get/576/gipi5-report.pdf/show_on_screen

The Guardian . (2016, 10 03). *UK exports small medium sized business sme*. Retrieved 07 02, 2018 from www.theguardian.com: https://www.theguardian.com/business/2016/oct/03/uk-exports-small-medium-sized-business-sme

The Guardian. (2015, 10 22). *Five steps to become the go-to expert in your field*. Retrieved 07 16, 2018 from www.theguardian.com : https://www.theguardian.com/small-business-network/2015/oct/27/become-go-to-expert-field-authority

The Guardian. (n.d.). *small business network*. Retrieved 07 22, 2018 from ttps://www.theguardian.com/small-business-network/2015/oct/14/small-business-advice-how-start-exporting-james-: www.theguardian.com

The Telegraph. (2015, 11 09). *Can the UK's SMEs be the engine for growth?* Retrieved 07 19, 2018 from www.telegraph.co.uk: https://www.telegraph.co.uk/business/sme-management/uk-sme-growth-insight/

The Telegraph. (n.d.). *Half of UK startups fail within 5 years*. Retrieved 07 02, 2018 from www.telegraph.co.uk: https://www.telegraph.co.uk/finance/businessclub/11174584/Half-of-UK-start-ups-fail-within-five-years.html

Thornton, K. B. (2012). *Our frugal future: Lessons from India's innovation system,*. Retrieved 07 22, 2018 from www.nesta.org.uk: http://www.nesta.org.uk/sites/default/files/our_frugal_future.pdf

Trade Ready. (2016). *Service Exports suddenly important* . Retrieved 07 02, 2018 from www.tradeready.ca: http://www.tradeready.ca/2016/trade-takeaways/service-exports-suddenly-important/

Trade Ready. (2016). *Service Exports suddenly important* . Retrieved 07 02, 2018 from www.tradeready.ca: http://www.tradeready.ca/2016/trade-takeaways/service-exports-suddenly-important/

Trade Ready. (2017). *You export strategy is* . Retrieved 07 22, 2018 from Trade Ready: http://www.tradeready.ca/2017/topics/market-entry-strategies/your-export-strategy-is-incomplete-without-these-4-things/

Tradeready.ca. (n.d.). *market-entry-strategies/use-10-international-trade-directories-find-next-partner-distributor/*. Retrieved 08 14, 2018 from http://www.tradeready.ca: http://www.tradeready.ca/2017/topics/market-entry-strategies/use-10-international-trade-directories-find-next-partner-distributor/

UK Government . (n.d.). *Preparing for our future* . Retrieved 07 02, 2018 from www.gov.uk: https://www.gov.uk/government/publications/preparing-for-our-future-uk-trade-policy/preparing-for-our-future-uk-trade-policy

UK Government. (n.d.). *SME supply chains exporters.* Retrieved 07 22, 2018 from https://assets.publishing.service.gov.uk: https://assets.publishing.service.gov.uk/government/uploads/system/uploads/attachment_data/file/524847/bis-16-230-smes-supply-chains-exporters.pdf wabccoaches. (n.d.). *power-responsibility-and-wisdom-exploring-the-issues-at-the-core-of-ethical-decision-making-and-leadership/*. Retrieved 08 14, 2018 from http://www.wabccoaches.com/blog

Webpresence digital. (n.d.). *small business digital agency*. Retrieved 07 02, 2018 from www.webpresence.digital: https://webpresence.digital/uk-blog/small-businesses-digital-agency/

World Bank. (n.d.). *micor businesses go global*. Retrieved 07 02, 2018 from www.worldbank.org: http://blogs.worldbank.org/jobs/psd/micro-businesses-go-global

www.80000hours.org. (n.d.). *www.80000hours.org*. Retrieved 07 22, 2018 from www.80000hours.org: www.80000hours.org

www.businessknowhow.com. (n.d.). *Startup business failure* . Retrieved 08 16, 2018 from business know how: https://www.businessknowhow.com/startup/business-failure.htm

www.entrepreneur.com. (n.d.). Retrieved 07 22, 2018 from www.entrepreneur.com: https://www.entrepreneur.com/article/253617

www.entrepreneur.com. (n.d.). Retrieved 07 22, 2018 from www.entrepreneur.com: https://www.entrepreneur.com/article/253617

www.forbes.com. (n.d.). *experts rule 15 ways*. Retrieved 07 22, 2018 from www.forbes.com: https://www.forbes.com/sites/work-in-progress/2012/01/27/experts-rule-15-ways-to-establish-authority-in-your-field/#2df41b88edf4

www.gov.uk/government/publications, U. G. (2018). *The future relationship between the United Kingdom and the European Union*. UK Parliament.

www.londonandzurich.co.uk. (n.d.). *www.londonandzurich.co.uk.* Retrieved 08 16, 2018 from much-late-payments-cost-business: https://www.londonandzurich.co.uk/much-late-payments-cost-business/

www.nature.com. (n.d.). Retrieved 07 22, 2018 from www.nature.com: https://www.nature.com/articles/461472a#ref1

www.nature.com. (n.d.). Retrieved 07 22, 2018 from www.nature.com: https://www.nature.com/articles/461472a#ref4

www.nature.com. (n.d.). *https://www.nature.com/articles/461472a#ref5* . Retrieved 07 22, 2018 from https://www.nature.com/articles/461472a#ref5 : https://www.nature.com/articles/461472a#ref5

www.thebalance.com/. (n.d.). *business marketing strategies.* Retrieved 07 22, 2018 from www.thebalance.com/: https://www.thebalance.com/business-marketing-strategies-2948337

Zaman, G. &. (1999). *Coexistenţa întreprinderilor mari şi mici, Tribuna Economică.* Retrieved 07 02, 2018 from www.mer.ase.ro: http://www.mer.ase.ro/files/2011-1/25.pdf

---

#0007 - 081118 - C1 - 210/148/8 - PB - 9781912243488